Two Sisters' Misguided Manual to Motherhood

Jamie E. Lightner

Jessica C. Warren

2 Sisters' Misguided Manual to Motherhood
Jamie E. Lightner & Jessica C. Warren

Copyright © 2014

All rights reserved, including the right to reproduce this book or portions thereof in any form whatsoever-except for brief quotation in printed reviews, without permission of the publisher.

Workbook pages created by Jamie Lightner & Dean Nixon of TurningLeaf Wellness Center

Design: Connection Graphics

Editors: Jamie L. Isham
Julie M. Metts

Publisher: Misguided Sisters, LLP
www.MisguidedSisters.com

Proofreaders: Rebecca Roberts, Amy Day, Kadren Hubbert, Reba Stafford, Laura Curfman

Library of Congress Control Number-2014908246

ISBN- 9780990357001 (paperback edition)

ISBN- 9780990357018 (ebook)

Disclaimer

This book is designed to provide information and motivation to our readers. It is sold with the understanding that the publisher is not engaged to render any type of psychological, legal, or any other kind of professional advice. The content of each article is the sole expression and opinion of its authors, and not necessarily that of the publisher. No warranties or guarantees are expressed or implied by the publisher's choice to include any of the content in this volume. Neither the publisher nor the individual author(s) shall be liable for any physical, psychological, emotional, financial, or commercial damages, including, but not limited to, special, incidental, consequential or other damages. Our views and rights are the same: You are responsible for your own choices, actions, and results.

Two Sisters' Misguided Manual to Motherhood

Jamie E. Lightner

Jessica C. Warren

Two Sisters' Acknowledgements written like an Oscar Acceptance Speech:

"Wow! Jess and I have so many people to thank. First of all we want to thank our amazing husbands. Oh, Jess, did you want to thank yours first?"

"You go ahead, 'Jame'. I'll follow."

"Okay. Babe, you are the best man I know. You complete me, you had me at hello, and I really would miss you if I never met you."

"Um, okay, 'Jame', you can't quote ALL your favorite chick flick lines, and I would like a turn before they start playing the music and boot us off the stage."

"Right. Sorry. Anyway, Michael, yes I am a sappy romantic, but you truly are amazing and I really wouldn't be who I am today without all your love, patience, and support. I love you more than words can say. Okay, go ahead, Jess."

"Jake, I couldn't have done any of this book without your amazing help! Not to mention you are the laughter in my life. If it weren't for you our children would be wrapped in bubble wrap and never allowed to leave the house. Love you more than you know!"

"We would also like to thank our kids: Josh, Kate, Timmy, Bo, Ayden, and Zayne. They truly are our inspiration. Without them, there would be no book. There would also be no dirty diapers, no messy house, no peanut butter sandwiches in the VCR, no therapy sessions…but I digress! We would also like to thank them for their patience while we took the time to write, even though it seemed, at times, we fed them frozen pizza three nights a week. (And one of those nights it was actually thawed!) We are blessed with amazing children and are so proud of each and every one of them.

We would also like to thank our amazing editor (Jamie Isham). She was able to read our minds and make sense of them on paper in the moments we couldn't. We now realize that behind every great author stands an even greater editor.

[Talking fast.] We would also like to thank our graphic designer firm (owner Connie Sweet of Connection Graphics). We not only appreciate her expertise, but we are also grateful for her patience and honesty as 2 crazy sisters dove into publishing. Thank goodness someone knew what they were doing.

"Oh, no kidding. That poor girl. 'Jame', remember when we almost…"

"Shhhh, don't give away all our mishaps. Let's try to hold on to what shred of dignity we may have left. Anyway, we would like to thank the whole Connection Graphics team. Lydia Calderon, graphic designer/ amazing book cover designer and the incredibly talented illustrator, John Strpko who depicted at least one crazy sister in the cover illustration."

"We would also like to thank our MANY proofreaders for taking the time to read our stories and at least pretend to like them. Rebecca Roberts, Amy Day, Kadren Hubbert, Reba Stafford, Laura Curfman."

"Well, not sure how much time we have left, but ok. We probably better wrap this up."

[Talking even faster.] "And of course we would like to thank our Mom (Julie) and our Dad (Jeff). They have been our biggest cheerleaders. They, for some strange reason, have believed in us the whole time. And on those days we thought we would never finish, they were there to encourage us to keep going. They both told us many times growing up that we would never understand just how much they loved us until we had kids of our own. They were right. And now that we understand, we would like to thank them for all their love and support."

"I hear the music starting, 'Jame'. I think they are trying to get us off the stage."

"I'm almost done, Jess. [Talking really, really fast.] I would like to thank Dean Nixon and TurningLeaf Seminars. It is because of the seminar experience and my training with them as a life coach that I feel I have the freedom to be human and can accept me for me. It's because of the principles they teach that I can create the exercises in this book.

Okay, Jess, I think that's it. Wow, they are playing that exit music REALLY loud. They must think we are talking too much."

"Well, 'Jame', our husbands have said that for years!"

"Just one more! I would also like to thank...."

Part 1
PMS: Perfect Mother Syndrome
Lessons in the Art of Being Human
A Challenge for You

Part 2
OMG...LMBO(Oh My Gosh...Laugh My Butt Off)
Laughing at Motherhood's Many Adventures
A Challenge for You

Part 3
Mommalicious
From Baby Bump to Muffin Top and Rockin' It
A Challenge for You

Part 4
I Need Chocolate...STAT
It's Just Been One of Those Days
A Challenge for You

Part 5
God Said He Wouldn't Put Me Through Anything I Couldn't Handle
Does He Have Me Confused with Someone Else?
A Challenge for You

Part 6
Why God Made Our Kids So Cute
So We Wouldn't Sell Them On Ebay
A Challenge for You

INTRODUCTION

This book is about

Well, I would like to start off by telling you what this book is NOT about. This book is not the "Kid 101" manual. This book will not guarantee that your kids won't argue, whine or make messes. This book is not a "how to potty train in 12 hours" book. If you are potty training while reading this book, I can almost guarantee you will still be potty training when you are done, especially if you have a boy. This book is not how to create the "perfect" kid, nor is it how to be a "perfect" parent. This is the book you read BEFORE you read all those "How-to" books. Because no matter what how-to book you read, no matter what discipline technique you use, and how consistent you are at using it...you will still have those crazy days when things aren't "manual" friendly. There will be days your precious angels aren't parent friendly, and definitely days when you, the parent, aren't kid friendly.

This parenting business is the worst, best, exhausting, most fulfilling, scary, chaotic, amazing job we will ever have. Time and time again, I have met parents who use the condition of their house, their kids' behavior, or other people's expectations as a "measuring stick" to determine whether or not they are a GOOD parent. I've been as guilty of this as anyone else at times. In fact, one day, I realized I had a chronic problem (and, no, it wasn't drinking, unless you count coffee!): I carried a "judgment" bat around and used it to beat myself up emotionally about everything, especially when it came to my parenting. I knew something needed to change, but I didn't know what, though I thought pills for depression might be a good start! Fortunately, I stumbled into a TurningLeaf seminar on emotional growth, and it was there that I began learning about "Value Based Parenting" and that I really didn't have to be perfect to be a GREAT mom! (And I came to terms with the fact that there would be days my husband would have NO clean underwear... and it would be OKAY.)

Not only was I hurting myself with my "measuring stick" mentality, but being so hard on myself was affecting the way my kids responded to me. When we create unrealistic expectations of ourselves that we can never measure up to, we feel SO beat-up that we don't have any energy left to actually parent. Our kids sense this negative energy, which magnifies the everyday challenges that come with simply raising kids. Instead, what if we learned to give ourselves some grace and laugh at the hilarious adventure of parenting?

I've been on this parenting journey for almost 15 years now, and let me tell ya, NO two kids are alike! Every child is different—some are more strong-willed than others—and there is NO "right" way of doing things. No magic formula. No manual for exactly how to parent in order to have a good kid. When I figured out I could stop judging myself for the mistakes

I made or my kids' embarrassing behavior and just recognize it all as part of a growth process for me and for them, I finally relaxed a little and really started to enjoy being a parent!

Five years ago, my sister had her first son and joined the parenting world. Together, we realized that one of the best ways to battle the harmful cycle of getting down on ourselves as parents, was to laugh and cry together as we shared the CRAZY adventures and mishaps that we often had with our kids. This book is a collection of many of our stories. We want you to know your kids are NOT the only ones making a scene in the store or throwing spaghetti at your head. You're not the only parent who fears your kids might need therapy when they're older or is tempted to sell them on Ebay at times.

So, it's time to put the "bat" down and start learning to laugh at life's mishaps! We invite you to witness our experience as perfectly imperfect moms—GOOD moms. We hope that by inviting you into our lives and sharing what we have learned along the way, you find encouragement, kinship, and maybe even some tools to help you feel good about you and enhance your "perfect" parenting abilities. We hope you take on the challenges we have given you at the end of each chapter. These are challenges that have helped us, personally, to put down the bat, accept ourselves, and love the experience of parenting with its many ups and downs. We invite you to laugh with us, cry with us, pull your hair out with us, and enjoy the candid stories of two sleep-deprived, coffee-filled, almost gripped-with-insanity, but perfectly imperfect moms!

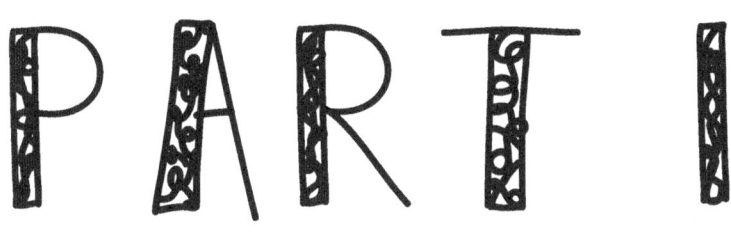

PMS: Perfect Mother Syndrome
Lessons in the art of being Human

As Time Goes On...

By Jamie

If you've been a parent for any length of time, you've already heard plenty of comments from other "concerned" parents, grandmas, check-out clerks, doctors, and any number of other people ranging from close family members to complete strangers who *ALL* feel they must tell you how to be the *PERFECT* parent to your little bundle of joy. I don't know about you, but my parenting approach seemed to change with each kid! At first, parenthood seemed an exciting, yet scary, new adventure. Then, somewhere down the road, I could barely remember a time when I was *NOT* a parent. The question is, did I become more at ease with parenting or, rather, was I so emotionally drained that I was just mentally and physically incapable of obtaining the recommended level of parent paranoia?

With my first-born son, I was *SO* regimented. I would heat his bottle for 38.7 seconds in the microwave, and if his pacifier fell to the floor it was *thoroughly* sanitized with soap and hot water. I also didn't allow him to be held by every set of arms in the room. To this day, I look back on my paranoia and I'm really not sure *WHY* I was so worried. Did I think he would break or contract a terminal disease? Was I concerned that he might experience social overload? Whatever I was afraid of with my first, I *CERTAINLY* got over it by the time kids number two, three, and four arrived! They got passed around so much there were times I wasn't exactly sure *WHO* might be holding them. I was pretty confident that if anyone ran off with them, eventually they would be looking for the return policy. And, I gotta say, with the third and fourth kid, if they didn't come back in 30 days or less with the receipt in hand, it was debatable whether or not they could collect a *FULL* refund! (Wink!)

With my *FIRST* kid, whenever any food landed on the floor it was sent off to a special laboratory for a safety inspection. By the time our second kid came along, we began to implement the five-second rule. Whenever a Cheerio hit the floor, we just picked it up and gave it right back to them, provided it was dry. Now, if it was a wet one, well of course we would inspect it first to make sure it hadn't picked up any foreign particles. By the time my third and fourth were toddlers, half the time I *DIDN'T* even have to cook lunch! They would scavenge the floor so well that the little snacks they found would hold them 'til dinner. Sometimes, there seemed to be enough to supply a three-course meal under the couch alone!

When I began leaving my *FIRST* kid with my husband I would tell him *EXACTLY* what to do. How to feed him and which way he liked to be burped, rocked, and put to sleep. I told him *EXACTLY* when to do everything. After the second kid came along I would just leave and say,

"Good luck," assuming that, no matter what, they would survive. By then, I just knew if I stayed in the house another consecutive day my sanity would *NOT* survive.

Granted, some of the details above have been dramatized for affect, but which ones have or haven't I am certainly *NOT* going to admit. While it may be true that, at times, I was too exhausted to reach the recommended level of paranoia, I believe I realized there was NO way for me to get this parenting thing perfectly right. It took several kids, crazy schedules, and insanely impossible demands on myself before I realized being a great mom isn't about getting all the answers right on the parenting exam. It isn't about making the *PERFECT* bottle or having the *PERFECT* schedule, or even making sure the kid doesn't ever eat a stale Cheerio. Rather than work so hard to be that *perfect* parent, let's relax, stop judging ourselves and others, and learn to enjoy our *PERFECTLY* unpredictable lives.

I am Smokin!
By Jessica

Today was an eventful day! Well, not really...it was just a regular day, but it *felt* eventful and I never even left the house. Have ya ever had those days where your head is so *FULL* of things that had to be done, but you simply didn't know *WHERE* to start? Ya know, those days when you just stood there in a daze, contemplating your to-do list, with items such as, yet not limited to, laundry, your grocery list, laundry, people you want to send notes to, laundry, gifts to mail, laundry, and a possible workout, not to mention the regular daily activities that simply accompany two kids?

Well, I was sure today was *NOT* going to be one of those "overwhelming" days. I woke up this morning feeling great, and I planned on being Wonder Woman! I had the house picked up, my first load of laundry in the washer, and my coffee in hand, ALL before my toddler even blinked his little eyes awake. It was beautiful outside, so I escaped to my back porch to steal a couple minutes to myself before my sleeping angels awoke. I began reading an insightful book, hoping to take some "me" time and gain a few morsels of encouragement for the day. As I started reading, my mind trailed off (a common problem I have). I found myself, once again, contemplating my to-do list. Rather than absorbing my "me" time, I was back in work mode, thinking of the things I needed to pick up at the store. I realized I was no longer in my Zen moment, so I took a deep breath and reminded myself that this was "ME" time and began reading again. I no sooner got through a paragraph and my mind wandered yet again. I started thinking of the letters I needed to write and the gifts I needed to mail. Oh, and my car was a mess, and I had to wash the stale bottle I noticed on the garage floor the other day and never picked up, which had probably become a living organism by now, and I don't even want to think about what it smelled like...*Oh right...I'm reading*, I reminded myself once again. I think I re-read the same paragraph about four times before I just decided to sit and think, seeing as extracting morsels from my book *WASN'T* happening. Let me tell ya, if I don't put boundaries on my thoughts I could sit all-day and spiral into a depressing hole. I'm just gonna let you in on my thought process in the hopes that some of you can relate. So here go my untethered thoughts...

...I should REALLY clean my baseboards (ugh!) and my bathroom floors need to be swept and mopped...gosh, what a ROTTEN housekeeper I am. My poor kids have to live in this NASTY house! I hate that I yelled at Ayden yesterday. I need to be more patient with my kids or they will grow up thinking yelling is an effective form of communication. How do I teach them how to be patient and calm when I haven't even learned how to do that MYSELF? Why am I a mom?!? I'm not cut out for this. I'm WAY too

selfish. I don't even want to THINK about how ridiculous I've been to my husband! How does he love me still? I'm so mean and he's SO great. And how does he still think I'm hot? Have you looked at yourself lately, Jess? I mean, REALLY, have you ever been fatter in your life? You used to be in such good shape. And now you can't tell where your love handles stop and your caboose begins!

Yup! That was my thought process when I let my mind trail off from my "inspirational" book. I wouldn't have thought it possible for me to end up in such a negative frame of mind, especially after how great my day started. Writing this and seeing everything on paper makes me realize even more how I need to put boundaries on my negative self-talk and then change the direction of my thoughts entirely. So when you find yourself entertaining the "dismals," I encourage you to change up everything in that moment. When your thoughts start to take you down, put on some music and have a dance party! Go blow up water balloons with your kids, fly like butterflies around the house, or visit the rainforest and jump like frogs. ANYTHING to change your thoughts in those moments. Once you have pulled yourself out of the downward spiral, replace all those negative thoughts with thoughts of gratitude and encouragement.

So after I pull myself out of MY downward spirals, this is what I choose to think...*I'm thankful I can have children, and that they are healthy and they know I love them. I'm thankful I make mistakes so my kids are gonna know it's okay for them to make mistakes. I'm thankful I don't have to be the perfect wife. My quirks are part of the reason my husband fell in love with me in the first place!* And try this one on: *Of course my husband thinks I'm hot...because I AM!...I am SMOKIN!!!!*

Then I usually put on a thong or something sexy and drop it like it's hot! Oh, *YEAH*! You can do anything to jumpstart yourself down a positive thinking path. It might feel *fake* in the beginning, but have *FUN* with it and do it *ENOUGH* to stay on top of your thoughts, and it will become second nature. Soon, you will notice powerful changes in your confidence and peace of mind. You won't yell as much, you won't stress about the house as much, and you'll simply start living life...a *HAPPY* life!

There is no right or wrong...
just Mom (and her gut)
By Jamie

I find it very interesting that, although we all know there really is no manual for parenting, we keep insisting we parent the "*RIGHT*" way. We all keep chasing that "pot of gold" at the end of the rainbow. I remember with my first baby, just learning to feed him the "*RIGHT*" way was quite the task.

When Josh was born, I was barely twenty years old. He was *SO* big! When his watermelon sized head burst through my lady parts, he did some damage, and *NOT* just *cosmetically*. I couldn't *WALK* or even lift my legs into bed without help for six weeks. I remember after about a week of feeding round the clock, day and night, every two hours (with my postpartum hormones raging), I was sitting on the edge of my bed looking at this little baby in the basinet with thoughts of inadequacy flooding my mind. I looked up at my mom, standing nearby, through tear-filled eyes and said, "I'm not *OLD* enough to be a mom!" Trying her best to hide her chuckle, "Oh really. How old are moms supposed to be?" she responded. "In their twenties," I said, with the tears now streaming down my face. "Honey, you *ARE* twenty," she said. "No, I mean you have to be twenty-*SOMETHING*!" I sobbed.

Being the awesome mom that she is, she completely overlooked my irrationality and insanity, sat down next to me, and put her arms around me. As we sat there on the bed she went on to say, "One day he will sleep through the night, and then he will crawl, and then he will walk, and before you know it he will be off to school." *Okay, maybe this isn't the end of the world*, I thought as she talked, and I began to calm down. It was hard to imagine my baby boy *EVER* growing up, but seeing that everyone else's kids did, I suppose mine probably would, too. So, for now, I would just feed him and believe I had whatever it took to figure out the next phase when it arrived.

Turns out, Josh was a *TRICKY* one! At about three weeks old he started crying and *DIDN'T* quit. After about two or three days of nursing constantly, and yet still he cried constantly, I began searching for answers. Well, what do ya know, the kid was just *STARVING*! I began supplementing him with some goat's milk and he began to sleep. (I know, I know, I am surprised I didn't get arrested! I can hear everyone now. "Huh, goats milk? What on *EARTH* were you thinking?!? I mean, is it FDA *approved*?!?") Well, when I was a baby I had a hard time with formula, so my mom used goat's milk and it worked great. I naturally followed in her footsteps. (Don't worry, the doctor informed me I didn't make the "*RIGHT*" choice.)

But my baby was sleeping and things were fine and dandy until one day my mom called me and told me some information she received from a friend. She said that my milk production was in correlation to how much water I was drinking, and *THAT* might be why I wasn't able to satisfy Josh. She also said that it wasn't too late to build my milk. I just needed to let the baby nurse as much as he wanted and I needed to drink *TONS* of water all day. Well, my mom-guilt kicked in and I thought I had a chance to get it *"RIGHT"* once again! I began what I call my "nursing marathon." I seriously nursed round the clock while I sat in my recliner watching movies. Occasionally, Josh would fall asleep and I would stick him in the bed only for him to wake up 15 minutes later, hungry *AGAIN*.

After two days and two nights of Josh's "all you can eat buffet", I headed into the hospital to talk with someone about my breastfeeding issues, because, "Every mom can make enough milk no matter the size of her breasts." (Ugh, if I had a dollar for every time I heard that, I could have hired someone to breastfeed *FOR* me!) I went into the hospital feeling like a total failure only to find out my baby didn't suck properly, therefore, he was not pulling enough milk to cause me to produce more. (At least that excuse worked for *THIS* kid!) That day at the hospital the nurse gave me a special bottle to help him learn how to suck and sent me home with a supplemental feeder and a breast pump that, I *swear*, weighed *MORE* than my car. (Those of you with breast pumps made in *this* century will have *NO* idea what I'm talking about here, but trust me, it was *HEAVY!*)

Seeing that I never had a machine sucking on my boobs before in my life, the pump was strange to me at first, but I got used to it after awhile. Yeah, sure, it did remind me of when I was a little girl and I would go down to the neighbor's dairy farm and watch them hook up the cows' utters. I was being milked in rather the same way…*SO* sexy.

While the pump was strange, the supplemental feeder was just plain *ANNOYING*. The idea was to hook the baby on to nurse and then slide this little tube with a small hole in the end into the corner of the baby's mouth. The other end of the tube was in a bottle full of formula. Keep in mind, I had to make sure the bottle was held high enough so the milk would run through it. I don't remember the *EXACT* science of how it all worked, but it was a job that required *FIVE* arms! Two for the baby, one for the bottle, one to slide the tube in the side of the baby's mouth, and one to pull up on the baby's cheek while trying to insert the tube. Supposedly, the baby would nurse to stimulate milk production, but would receive formula at the same time. And as my milk production got better, less formula would be sucked from the tube.

Perhaps I would be better at explaining the engineering behind how this supplemental feeding contraption worked if I had actually *experienced* it *WORKING*. I finally just quit the whole supplementing contraption and pumped after every time Josh nursed to build my milk. Just keeping up with that schedule was a *FIASCO* of its own! Our feeding basically looked like this: Josh would wake and I would nurse for ten minutes on both sides. (I did this because "the experts" say nursing a baby is the best way to stimulate your milk production.) Then I would change his diaper, heat up a bottle, and feed him formula 'til he was actually full. Next, I would put him to bed and go use the breast pump for ten minutes to further build my milk supply. So the whole process took just about an hour, and then he was back up one hour later to do it *ALL OVER AGAIN*.

After a few weeks of this, my husband noticed the insanity slowly taking over my personality. He finally just came home from work one day and said, "You are done nursing today." I know that might sound domineering, however my husband is anything *BUT* domineering. He had supported me the whole time, but he realized it was taking its toll on me and the *ONLY* reason I wouldn't just give up was because I felt *GUILTY*. I believed that to be a good mom, I had to breastfeed my baby, and since "every mom can produce enough milk for her baby no matter the size of the breasts," well, I had to keep working until I got it "RIGHT"! That day my husband said to me, "Jamie, *I* will be the bad guy. You don't have to feel *guilty*. You can just blame it on your mean husband ordering you to quit nursing." I actually felt *INCREDIBLY* relieved as he said those words to me. I began to think of what it would be like to just feed Josh once every few hours and not have to feed a pump, too!

So, after Michael *ordered* me to quite nursing, we came up with a solution that we both felt good about. I simply nursed him 'til he drained each breast, because I really did enjoy nursing, and then I would follow with a bottle to be sure he was full. Gradually, as my milk supply diminished, he nursed for shorter periods of time and drank more from the bottle until I just quit nursing all together, but it was *STRESS-FREE*! When I was unable to satisfy my following three kids with solely breast milk, I began supplementing with formula the same way I did with Josh. I made peace with the fact that if "all moms make enough milk no matter the breast size," well then I must do it *"wrong"* every single time, and I just *DON'T CARE* anymore. I gave my baby as much breast milk as I could and then moved on to a bottle of that manmade stuff that, frankly, helped my babies sleep! And to be quite honest, if I didn't *EVENTUALLY* get some sleep, successful breastfeeding was going to be the *LEAST* of my problems. (I did find a formula that both the doctor and I approved, and I count that a success.)

It was through this experience with Josh that I realized, I could *glean* from other moms, but ultimately I was going to have to create my *OWN* parenting manual. After having four kids, there is one thing I am sure of, and that is there are *NO* two kids alike! I could create a manual for each one of them, and even then, it is likely to change as they grow. The only way to survive motherhood is to throw out your expectations and the expectations of everyone else, which for some reason we all seem to care *WAY* too much about. Just *THROW* them all out! *LOVE* your kid with all your heart and don't ever underestimate your "mom gut."

I am a firm believer in the "mom gut". God gave it to moms because they don't sell the exact manual for your kid on the shelves of a bookstore. *YOU* know your own kid better than anyone else. Yes, you will make mistakes along the way, but you pick yourself up, say a few "I'm sorrys" and then let your love fill in the gaps. As a mom of four, I still find myself trying to raise my kids *"RIGHT"* and I work at creating this perfect child to reflect my wonderful parenting abilities. But our children are just as human as *WE* are, and they will *EACH* have their own personalities and phases. So you might as well stop trying to be *"RIGHT"* and just be...**Mom.**

Do your best...what?!?!

By Jamie

What is your best? All throughout life we hear the common phrase, "Just do your best." Well, for those of us who are perfectionists, this concept gets hazy, 'cause there is always, *I could have done better.* Ya know how it goes: *I could have worked harder, I could have worked longer.* Then, when we throw this concept into the parenting arena, we are wondering how much therapy our kids are going to need by the time they are twenty, 'cause, *I could have done it better!*

As parents, we want to do a *GOOD* job of raising our kids. We want them to know we love them. We want to be a patient teacher to them.

We want to have tea parties and play Legos, all the while teaching them values that will help them throughout their entire lives. We want to teach them responsibility, respect, love, and compassion. Naturally, we are not perfect, and as we see ourselves falling short of our *"BEST"* expectations of ourselves, we begin a destructive cycle of guilt and never feeling like we are *ENOUGH*.

For example your day might look like this...

You were up at 1:00am with a crying baby and up again at 3:00am with a kid who insisted there was a monster in his closet. Finally, at 4:00am all were sleeping once again, only to have your alarm ring at 6:30am to begin your day. You drag yourself out of bed, doing your *"BEST"* to be bright-eyed and bushy-tailed, getting your six-year-old and eight-year-old out the door to school, but you feel like a truck hit you, so rather than make them a warm bowl of oatmeal like all the parents who do their *"BEST"* do, you throw a bowl of stale Captain Crunch in front of them. Now, the stale factor is not actually your fault, 'cause the kids keep leaving the bag of cereal open when they put the box away. But it inevitably *becomes* your fault as you tell yourself you need to do a *BETTER* job of teaching your kids how to clean up after breakfast. I mean, *HOW* are they going to keep a job someday if you haven't even succeeded in getting them to routinely fold down the cereal bag? Finally, with a kiss planted on their cheeks, you send them out the door at 7:30 to catch their ride. Then you run back to your bed as fast as you can, hoping your three-year-old and ten-month-old sleep at least *ONE* more hour. You lie there trying to catch up on some lost sleep, but in the back of your mind, your "Do Your Best Sergeant" is chanting, *"Laundry! Dishes! Toilets! Don't forget to mop the floor so when the baby eats off of it today you won't feel as bad!"* Your body's need for sleep wins *THIS* battle, but the feelings of inadequacy are still there when you wake. Your three-year-old pulls you out of bed after you finally quit thinking long enough to sleep for just 20 minutes. Again, stale Captain

Crunch is on the breakfast menu. Afterwards, while you are cleaning up the breakfast mess, you feel guilty for yelling at your daughter when she stuck her elbow in her bowl, dumping it all over. *NOW* you are telling yourself how you need to be a patient mom who doesn't "yell over spilt milk". The rest of the day is filled with a couple tea parties with your toddler and lots of household chores, that is, when the baby doesn't insist he be front and center. That afternoon, when the "sacred" naptime is almost near, you clean up the smeared jelly on the table from lunch and you begin to make the *IMPOSSIBLE* list of all the chores you intend on finishing while the kids sleep. Later that afternoon, you load the younger kids into the van and go pick up your older kids from school. The rest of the afternoon is filled with more chores, keeping the baby out of the toilet, putting your three-year-old in time-out for coloring on the walls, and convincing your first-grader that it is against the law to make water balloons inside the house, *ALL* while somehow managing to cook dinner and wash a load or two of laundry so your husband will have clean underwear to put on before work tomorrow. Oh, and then it is off to the little league game at 7:00pm! After the game, the evening is filled with dinner cleanup, followed by baths and a bedtime story. You kiss the kids goodnight and tuck them in three times, 'cause they need to go potty, get their *OTHER* favorite teddy bear, or tell you about an owie they *JUST* discovered on their finger. Once tucked away for sure, you throw a load of laundry in the dryer. As you collapse into bed, your "Do Your Best" sergeant orders, *"You need to be MORE patient! You need to have more tea parties! You need to keep a cleaner floor and DEFINITELY cleaner toilets! You need to read more stories! You obviously aren't doing your "BEST", because you can do BETTER!"*

Now, obviously, your day may not look *EXACTLY* like the scene above, but I'm sure many of you can relate to the demands of parenthood. I remember, when my kids were babies, I would feel guilty for napping when they would nap. I thought I should be doing housework, or better yet, reading my Bible or some inspirational book that taught me how to be a better person. But the fact of the matter was, what I really *NEEDED* in that moment in order to be my true *"BEST"*... was a nap!!!

So, I challenge you to redefine your *"BEST."* Look at yourself honestly and have end goals rather than expectations. *EXPECTATIONS* require perfection and instantaneous results. *GOALS* require commitment to progression, but take *TIME*. And if you're making progress toward your goals, don't beat yourself up about the rest—that will only hold you back. And seriously, set *REALISTIC* goals....not goals that only parents who don't require sleep can accomplish! And in those moments of "yelling over spilt milk", go back and teach your kids one of the most valuable lessons they can learn, and that is how to say, "I am sorry." Our kids learn the most by example. So, yes, do your best! My definition of doing my *"BEST"* is simply this: learn from yesterday, accept who I am today, while growing and progressing as the future days unfold.

I am human... and that's okay
By Jamie

I am finding myself asking the question, "*WHY* do we struggle with our humanity?" It is perplexing to me that we are *ALL* human, yet we all strive to be *SUPER*-human. All the superhero movies are not too far from what we wish we were and attempt to be. We may recognize the fact that we aren't bulletproof and we don't have x-ray vision, but we all want to essentially have bulletproof character and emotions and be able to see through every moment to the best way to handle any situation.

I, myself, try to be *WONDER WOMAN*. I find myself striving to be the mom that has it all together. The mom that doesn't forget lunches, fieldtrips, or appointments. The mom that is never late and arrives with each kid showered and no dirt under their fingernails. (Let's not even talk about the *length* of those fingernails which sometimes remind me of Edward Scissorhands by the time I notice they need a trim!) I want to be the mom who is never impatient and always knows what to tell her children when they are down. I want to be the perfect wife, with dinner on the table and a smile on my face. (Yeah, my husband would probably love that, too! Some days we have *WHATEVER* we can find in the fridge. I call it, "If it's not Moldy, Eat it for Dinner" Day.) I want to be that perfect friend who never lets anyone down and *NEVER* says anything stupid. **And one day I realized I was striving for PERFECTION**. My search for perfection wasn't some quest to be holier-than-thou, but to be the *BEST* I could be, not necessarily for me, but for everyone *ELSE*. Yet, in that moment, I knew that perfection, just like tomorrow, would *NEVER* come.

However, what I am beginning to realize is, I *AM* perfect. I am a perfect human being, learning and growing every day. I am a human being who, at times, struggles with depression or yells at my kids. I sometimes cry over stupid stuff. The truth is, I *AM* going to let people down, and I'm learning, that is *OKAY*. We all learn from our imperfections, which is *TOTALLY* perfect. I learn from my mistakes (*eventually*!), and others will learn from my mistakes as well.

I need to accept that I am *NOT* Wonder Woman, and forgetting a lunch or burning dinner is going to happen. I may discover their astonishingly dirty, long nails while sending them out the door at the last second to catch the bus and have no time to do anything about it. Or, even worse, I am going to come up short emotionally for my kids.

When I am at odds with my own humanity, I unintentionally rob myself of enjoying and living life. For instance, today I was cranky with the kids. I was irritated over chores left undone and snapped at them for toys left out. When they didn't listen, I responded with very short words and irritated tones. I could feel the *CRANKY* energy just oozing off of me and it was *NOT* pretty. Bo had decided to quit being potty trained and I was not shy about showing my disappointment! Josh and Kate were exercising their rights as "pre-teens", and Timmy was determined to put Bo in his newfound wrestling moves. Each time I addressed the kids I would get upset, and I felt justified because *THEY* were not listening and had been told a *MILLION* times.

At the end of days like this, though, I feel remorse. I find myself wishing I had been more patient, more like the "Kid Whisperer", because at the end of the day, very little of the stuff I ranted about *MATTERS* anymore. I just want them to know that I love them and I am proud of everything they are learning.

It is at this point in time that I have a *CHOICE* to make. I can either feel *GUILTY* for all my shortcomings as a parent or I can *LEARN* from my mistakes, lay my head down for the night, and start all over again tomorrow. **'Cause frankly, I am a *DANG* good mom**. I love my kids so much that to think of them creates a lump in my throat and a pang in my heart. It is in moments like these, the very best I can be for them is "human." To be a mom who bleeds and knows how to say, "I am sorry." To be a mom who, despite all my shortcomings, is determined as heck to keep moving forward. To be a mom who may get knocked down, but pulls herself right back up.

It is times like these I humble myself before my Creator and thank Him for all He has given me, and all He teaches me every day. Life is too short to spend so much time not accepting our *HUMANITY*.

To judge or not to judge?... Neither!! Just be yourself.
By Jamie

If I have to be "*RIGHT*" then *THEY* have to be "*WRONG*", which leaves me always judging. And if I am judging others, then I am susceptible to the judgments of others. But if I accept me as *ME*, not right or wrong, I now have the ability to accept *OTHERS* exactly as they are. When I accept that my *METHODS* may be different from theirs, I can now respect their methods, rather than be offended. When I accept that my *BAGGAGE* and *HURTS* affect my reactions, then I can understand that others have their own different baggage and hurts dictating their reactions. When I accept what appears to be "*different*" externally, it gives me the ability to see that at the depth of our souls, we are all the same.

We all love, we all bleed, and we all just want to feel of value in this life. We all work SO hard not to get hurt by someone else, or rather feel de-valued by someone else. But the key is, as we learn to value ourselves, mistakes and all, then we will stop judging ourselves. When we stop *JUDGING* ourselves, then we will no longer feel the need to *PROTECT* ourselves. When we no longer feel the need to protect ourselves, we become *IMPASSIVE* to others' judgments of us.

The first step is to truly believe that by just breathing on this earth, we are *ALL* of value and worthy of life because our maker gave it to us. When we truly **KNOW** this, then we will no longer worry that someone will take it away, because the thought will not even cross our minds—the possibility no longer exists. As we accept ourselves, the existence of judgment just fades away.

So today, I challenge you to accept yourself, "*flaws*" and all, because I guarantee if you look closely at your so-called "*flaws*", you will find they have been refining tools that have made you into the *DIAMOND* you truly are.

A challenge for you: "Stop PMS-ing"

Ya know, sometimes we need to remind ourselves of just how *AWESOME* we really are. Even though this chapter was about accepting our humanity, I am not simply referring to our imperfections. It is important to acknowledge our "*AWESOMENESS*" as well! Oftentimes, we tend to focus primarily on the areas we need to improve and we neglect to recognize the areas in which we are commendable. When we take ownership of our "*AWESOMENESS*", this gives us the confidence and energy needed to make the commitments necessary for progression. So today, I challenge you to recognize both.

If you can't think of anything, ask your kids or a friend who most likely thinks more highly of you than you think of yourself.

"Stop PMS-ing" Challenge: Part 1

List 3 attributes, of your parenting, in which you are AWESOME!

Example...I am *AWESOME* at letting my kids know they are Loved!

1.

_____

2.

_____

3.

_____

**I not only challenge you to read your statements above, every day for a week, I also challenge you to BELIEVE them.

"Stop PMS-ing" Challenge: Part 2

Set a goal and implement an idea where you would like to see improvement.

Example: I would like to spend more time together as a family. I am going to create Family Game Night once a month.

PART 2

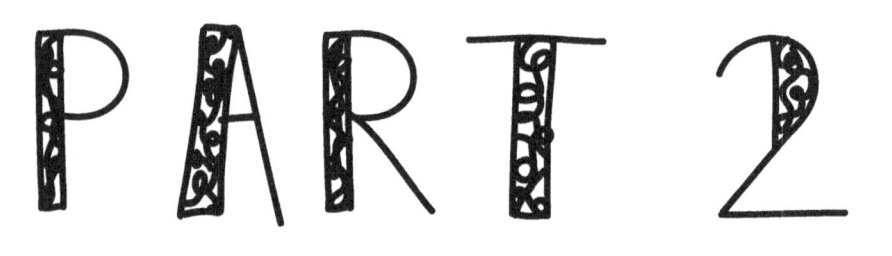

OMG...LMBO
(Oh My Gosh...Laugh My Butt Off)
Laughing at motherhood's
many adventures

Mom down! We have a MOM DOWN!

By Jessica

Grocery shopping with toddlers can be a *BIT* scary, so I called Jamie this morning to see if she wanted to keep me company. Since she had some errands to run herself, she agreed. Being the savvy mom that I am, I made some cinnamon muffins and hoped they would keep the kids happy throughout all the stops we had to make. Our first stop was returning a couple of items to one store, followed by a visit to the consignment shop, and then came the last stop of the day: the local warehouse store, where we could buy groceries in bulk and save our pennies! It seems anywhere Jamie and I go, we tend to make a scene, but I was confident today would be different because we were doing *GREAT.*

Slightly tired and exhausted from scratching off most of the items on our to-do list, we entered the warehouse with "the Kid on Red Bull" (Bo) followed by his "Little Prototype" (Ayden), while I carried "Chunky Buns" (Zayne). I was secretly hoping for a bath later to relieve the backache I was feeling as I hauled him around. I'm sure we were a *SIGHT* throughout the *WHOLE* store! Ayden and Bo didn't want to be separated, so all over the warehouse people kept hearing Jamie or me holler at one of them. "Keep up boys!"...."Ayden, are you staying with me or Aunt 'Mame'?"...."Bo, you need to listen!"

Jamie and I finally met up in the freezer section where she began telling me how "Aunt Flow" was wreaking havoc on her lady parts and she didn't know how much longer she could shop. I felt bad for her, sure, but I was *DETERMINED* to finish. *I didn't haul my two kids out in 10-degree weather just to grab HALF my list!* Her lady problems would have to wait. She pushed her cart a couple of steps in front of me and stopped. Holding her stomach, she looked back at me and gasped, "I'm *NOT* okay..Oh, my gosh! It *REALLY* hurts!"

Not really feeling the urgency of the moment, I opened up a bag of veggie straws and started feeding them to my whiny eighteen-month-old, Zayne. "What do you want me to *DO*?" was my less than empathetic response to her, as I stuffed a chip in my own mouth. Then she *SAT* down *RIGHT THERE* in the middle of the aisle and turned white as a ghost! *Wow, she really isn't okay*, I thought to myself. *What am I going to do with two carts and three children if she decides to pass out on me?* At that moment, a man walked over and asked her if she was alright and if she needed anything. "Ugh...I'm *FINE!*" she snapped. "I just need to sit for a minute," was her annoyed response, as she waved him off with one hand and held her head with the other! (She gets a *LITTLE* grouchy when she is in pain. *DON'T* even get me started on her labor and delivery stories!) Figuring I needed to assist her in making a quick exit, I gave her the keys to my car and she hobbled toward the doors.

So there I was, with both carts full of food and three starving, cranky kids, one of them being Bo. I tried to remember what was on Jamie's list, knowing she wouldn't want to leave without at least *SOME* of what she came for. I knew she needed cheese and pizza, so we headed toward the dairy aisle. We found ourselves passing all the wonderful samples, strawberries among them. Ayden asked me if we could get one and I calmly tried to tell him no, that Aunt "Mame" didn't feel good so we had to hurry. Out of the blue, I heard Bo's voice plow its way through my conversation and blast, "SHTWAABERRIES!" You would have thought the kid saw Santa Claus!

"I WANT SOME SHTWAABERRIES!"

His declaration doused me with enough of his *SPIT* to hydrate a small dog! Wiping away the overspray, I looked at him bug-eyed, wondering how he could be so LOUD. Trying to reasonably explain myself, I plopped a frozen pizza in the cart and said, "No, honey, your mommy doesn't feel..."

"AUNT '*JESHEE*', I WANT SOME SHTWAABERRIES!" he shouted.

It was as if I *wasn't* even talking. After grabbing the pizza, I was "choo-choo-train-ing" myself and the two carts toward the cheese and, unfortunately, had to pass the lovely strawberries again.

> Tell yourself you're awesome

"SHTWABERRIES!" Bo yelled again, as if the whole store didn't hear him the *FIRST* two times.

"No, Bo!" I thought maybe, if I simplified my answer, he might understand better. *NOPE*! He kept asking, so I decided to ignore him. I grabbed the cheese and tried to go down my mental grocery list again when a lady approached me and asked, "Are you the sister of the girl..." I didn't hear the last of her sentence because of the pudgy little boy in my cart who, apparently, *STILL* wanted "*SHTWAABERRIES!*" I nodded my head knowing it had to be Jamie. Then over the loudspeaker I heard, "Would Jessica, the sister of Jamie, please come to the exit?"

Oh, my gosh! I thought to myself. *"Did she get hit by a car on her way out?!?"* The lady looked at me sympathetically and proceeded to say, "She collapsed...but it's okay, she is talking now. Do you want me to stay with the kids while you go check on her?" My first thought was *OH @#$!....she freakin' fainted! What a GREAT sister I am! Sending her to the car thinking it's just menstrual, and she freakin' fainted*! My second thought was, *Leave my kids with you?..Over my DEAD BODY*! (Don't get me wrong, I believe that there are lots of good people in this world; I just wouldn't use *MY* kids to figure out if *THIS* lady was one of them.) I felt beads of sweat start to form on my upper lip and in the small of my back as I grabbed all three of, what now felt like, all my *OWN* kids.

I hurriedly apologized for the opened bag of chips, abandoned my two carts full of groceries, and headed for the exit. I carried "Chunky Buns", held Ayden's hand, and had to argue with Bo about *WHY* he had to hold Ayden's other hand. As I made my way to the front of the store, I thought to myself, *Knowing my sister, she will be fine and then she will be bummed I didn't just check out so we didn't head home empty-handed.*

When I approached the scene, I saw four people forming a circle around Jamie and asking questions. Once I knew she was okay, I had to hold back the *LAUGHTER*! She was slumped over on the concrete, apparently irritated that they wouldn't leave her alone. I heard one man ask her if she was diabetic. "NO! I am *NOT* a diabetic!" she snapped back. *Yup, time to get her in the car and away from these people before she embarrasses herself.* I made my way to her side and let her know I was going to load the kids and pull around to pick her up. She started crying once she saw me, and I paused. I knew she just wanted to LEAVE, and I could hardly even console her with our three chitlins hanging off of me!

One lady offered to hold Zayne and I politely declined, looking at her as though she wasn't qualified. Another man piped up and said, "Okay, an ambulance is on the way."

Jamie almost *LOST* it! "WELL, CALL THEM AND TELL THEM TO *TURN* AROUND. I AM **NOT** PAYING **THAT** BILL!!!"

She kept hollering something at them while a man pulled me aside. His face was full of concern as he said, "This isn't right. You don't collapse on a concrete walkway and say you're fine." I could still hear my sister in the background, now sounding like an elderly escapee from a senior home!

"I know. I'll get her in the car and we'll head to the hospital," I said, knowing it would put everyone at ease and then we could easily slip away. I corralled all of the kids and got them loaded and buckled while answering several of Bo's questions in the process. Then I remembered, *I gave Jamie the keys earlier in the store*! I kept my eye on the car while I *RAN* up to her and grabbed them, then *RAN* back and pulled the car up in *JUST* enough time to see the paramedic taking her blood pressure. *Oh, boy*! I didn't want anyone *POKING* the bear, so I quickly jumped out and said, "Okay! I got it from here. Let's get you loaded!"

But, before I could bend down to help her up, the paramedic stopped me and said, "I will let your sister go with you as long as you're going *straight* to the hospital."

I started to shake my head in *fake* agreement when I heard my sister protesting from her slumped position on the sidewalk. "HECK NO! I'm not going to the hospital! This is just *GIRL* problems! I'm going to go home, pop six ibuprofen, and lay down with a hot water bottle!"

I gave Jamie a look to let her know she *WASN'T* helping the situation. I'm sure everyone already thought she was on some *STRONG* meds. So, I *quietly* (without letting Jamie hear me) said to the medic, "Yeah, I'll get her there," with a reassuring nod.

After I finally stole her away from the medical professionals, I drove across the street to the gas station, where I ran in and grabbed pain reliever and a bottle of water. Jamie took a couple, and by the time we got home she was her cheery little self again and we were laughing at the turn of events that had happened. *And I was hoping we wouldn't* *make a scene **today**.* I just *HAD* to chuckle when she said with a smile, "I was *FINE.* You shoulda just checked out and *THEN* rescued me. At least then we would have food for the week!"

(After visiting the doctor, Jamie found out she was anemic and it actually WAS kind of serious. That's why she was getting lightheaded when she had menstrual cramps. A couple months on an iron supplement and she was good as new!)

What part of the word camping says *VACATION?*

By Jamie

My husband grew up camping. As a kid I was fascinated by the idea, but had never actually been *camping*. While we were dating, I camped with Michael and his family several times and loved it. I *even* camped when I was pregnant and again when I had two kids! However, by the time we had our third and fourth kid, I was *NOT* so fond of the idea. So, needless to say, our camping days came to a grim halt. Whenever my husband would suggest we go camping, I would just look at him and say, "Honey,

WHY would I go on "vacation" to work *harder* than I do at home?"

You see, my idea of a vacation is going somewhere the beds already have sheets on them and are magically made for you every day when you are not looking. Packing my own bedding and mattress, only to assemble them in a tent in which I can't even stand up straight? Yeah, *NOT* sounding very *vacation-ish.*

My ideal vacation does not involve carrying soap and shampoo down the path to take a shower in what would *hopefully* be AT LEAST warm water, while being sure my flip flops remain on my feet at *ALL* times ('cause have you seen the floors in those camp showers?!?).

My ideal vacation does not involve stumbling across the grassy way with a flashlight in my hand just to "tinkle" *IN THE MIDDLE OF THE NIGHT*, not to mention having to take the time to line the toilet seat with toilet paper at 3:00 am because I'm never sure whether that wet seat is a result of the overzealously flushing toilets or some little person's inability to aim. Or, better yet, *WHY* would I want to escort my *KIDS* to the bathroom? At home they handle all that themselves; I barely hear the toilet flush!

Oh, yes, and while I am discussing such camping fun, as if dishes aren't annoying enough to wash with electricity and hot water! Why don't we wash them in a bucket of COLD water that we have to haul *BY HAND* from *WHEREVER* the nearest spout is? Hmmmm, I just can't wait.

Well, when Michael's family planned a "family" camping trip just 35 minutes from my house, I came up with the best camping solution *EVER!* It involved warm water, my own private restroom, and a *GOOD* night's rest. Yup, you guessed it! Michael took our three oldest kids and "roughed it", while the toddler and I decided to be "day campers". We joined the family at the campsite during the day, had our camping fun, swam at the beach and roasted marshmallows, and went home when everyone else made their evening trek to the bathrooms across the campground. I slept in a cool, comfy bed in a room about 70 degrees, listening to the *hummmm* of my ceiling fan. Mike and the kids? Well, they were sleeping in a bed of sand, in a room of 85 degrees, listening to the *hummmm* of mosquitoes looking for a midnight snack. And from the looks of all of them when I arrived back at camp the next day, they were the *BUFFET* of choice!

Smell my Finger
By Jessica

Before I became a parent (famous last words, I know), I *NEVER* thought I would experience the *CRAZY* stories of parenthood I often heard from my friends. They always told these dramatic stories of children who painted the walls with their poop, or kids who ate a marble and the parents had to dig through fecal matter for days trying to see if it passed. By the time my son was two years old, he hadn't done anything too incredibly disgusting, and I began to thank God that he was *NOT* dramatic. (I obviously hadn't learned my lesson, yet, because every time I get cocky about my well-behaved little boy I start to see a new side of him!)

One particular day, I was washing dishes, and in walked my little towhead. He had a goofy look on his face, a sure sign that I should investigate.

"What's up bud?" I asked. He lifted up his arm and attempted to reach my nose with his little pointer finger.

"Smell my finger," he said, with a mischievous grin on his face.

Confused and a little grossed out, considering I've seen the *MANY* uses that little finger had, I laughed and said, "No. Why?"

"Smell it," he insisted, standing on his tippy toes in hopes to get his finger closer.

"No! What *is* it?" I exclaimed, wrinkling my nose in disgust.

His face lit up as he said, "It's my poop!" *Yuck!* The way he said it was almost as though he was amazed at how that smell could go from his butt to his finger. Then he proceeded to say, "See mom, I show you," and he reached around to shove his hand down his pants once again. I stopped him, of course, and had the "That's Disgusting" talk. As *GROSS* as it was, though, I *HAD* to laugh.

Later that day, I was folding laundry and our dog was lying on the floor beside me. I watched my son, who was just across the room, play with three pennies in his hand. *He is so adorable the way he carries around his little trinkets*, I thought. Then he got up and walked over to the dog, eyeballing him as though he had a plan. He looked at his pennies, and then looked at our dog's butt. No sooner did he get one penny clasped with his pointer and thumb, he started for our dog's chocolate starfish! I JUMPED over to him and grabbed his pennies, exclaiming, "Absolutely NOT!!!" I guess we will have to go over the "That's Disgusting" talk ONE more time!

Mr. Mom

By Jessica

My husband had to be Mr. Mom for three days. I was away, and he took some time off work to hold down the fort. I figured he would pass with flying colors (which he did), however I *MUST* admit, I was hoping the boys would be their *ENERGETIC* selves! I wanted Jake to get a small taste of day-to-day life as the sole parent responsible for our boys, so I even asked him to keep the house as tidy as possible. I wasn't expecting him to scrub toilets or do laundry, just clean up after meals and pick up toys at the end of the day.

When I first began hearing of some of the difficulties he was facing, I didn't feel bad for him *AT ALL*. As he told me his woes of Zayne being *whiny*, Ayden *hitting* his brother, and the *nasty* diaper explosions, I couldn't help but think it sounded like an *AVERAGE* day to me! It was hard to feel bad for him when I do this sort of thing day in and day out... *EVERY...SINGLE...DAY.*

Well *THAT* was until I heard about day *THREE*, when Jake got a taste of motherhood at *FULL* throttle! He had given Ayden, our three-year-old, a glass of Emergen-C after dinner. (For those of you who don't know what that is, it's a vitamin C drink that is as carbonated as cola.) After Ayden chugged it down, he began playing chase with his brother. When Zayne tired of the endless running, he went to his usual place when he gets bored—my pantry. He grabbed a bag of brown rice that happened to be opened, and when Jake walked in the room Zayne was shaking the bag around and dispersing rice all over. Jake snatched the rice from his hands and reached for the broom to begin cleaning up Zayne's "floor art".

While sweeping the rice, a very carbonated Ayden flew into the kitchen and *STOPPED* abruptly. "Daddy...I don't feel...*BLAAAAH!*" He *PUKED* all over the floor! My husband discovered firsthand that letting a three-year-old have a fizzy drink and then chase his brother in circles is like shaking a can of pop and opening it right away. Jake *GRABBED* Ayden and did the "Superman fly" to the bathroom. "Puke in the toilet, buddy!" Jake stressed. Ayden reached up for the toilet paper roll sitting on the back of the toilet. While pulling some tissue off the roll to wipe his face, he began puking again and dropped the *WHOLE* roll right into the puke-filled toilet! After wiping Ayden up and making sure he was okay, Jake went back out into the kitchen to find Zayne on all fours, pushing the spilt rice into the orange puddle of *PUKE*! It was at this point in time that Jake called me and simply said, "I need you!" Even though I couldn't come home, I appreciated him admitting that being a mom is *NOT* an easy job. He managed to recover without me and even had the house clean and both little kiddos asleep in their beds by the time

I returned later. *WHAT* a man! He's such a great Mr. Mom, I think I'll start planning my next trip! (*Wink!*)

Bathrooms with Boys...oh, BOY!

By Jamie

"Put the seat up before you pee! Then put it back down when you are done!" I said for the *MILLIONTH* time in my career as a mom. Boys and bathrooms...what an *adventure*!

Throughout my years of raising boys, I have often walked into my bathroom greeted by the *lovely* aroma of a giant urinal. Now, I'm not suggesting that I hadn't cleaned my bathroom for weeks and *consequently* it began to smell. (Well, that *DID* happen on occasion, and how often, I'd rather *NOT* say. That information is *FAR* too incriminating to just hand out.) However, just two days after each time I *THOROUGHLY* scrubbed my bathroom with bleach, the urinal smell kept returning.

Naturally, I figured out that this was because my boys all came with their own personal squirt gun. And the problem is this squirt gun did *NOT* come with a scope! I have noticed the ability to aim without a scope is *SERIOUSLY* limited, and it is crazy *WHERE* the stream lands.

One particular time, I sat on the toilet seat only to feel a *not-so-pleasant* wet sensation against my *CHEEKS*! Now, considering the fact that I didn't have a bidet, my only hope was that a freshly showered kid sat on the seat with their clean, *wet* butt. However, then I remembered that just before I stepped into the bathroom I was looking at my sweaty, grubby kids thinking, *Eeeeeww, you all need showers*, which shattered *ALL* hopes of the wet sensation being a *SANITARY* one. Then my mind wandered to all the times I had seen my boys hitting the *BACK* of the toilet seat before shifting things downward. It was pretty obvious that, there I was, *SITTING IN LITTLE BOY TINKLE SPLATTER. Yuck!* After I disinfected myself *AND* the seat, I noticed the puddle that had collected on the floor beside the toilet. I was sure *THAT* wasn't helping the smell, either.

As I washed my hands, I notice my trashcan had splatter running down the side of it. I tried to convince myself there were *MANY* explanations for that. It could be opening up a pop can after it was dropped… um, near the toilet? Or, maybe it was a squirt gun fight in the bathroom. Now *THAT* is quite probable, only I believe the water would have evaporated, not turned into a sticky, gross, goo running down the side of my trash can. *SERIOUSLY, how* do they get it *EVERYWHERE*?

Well, some of my questions were answered one day while I was standing at my vanity doing my hair. My five-year-old son, Timmy, walked in to go potty. He was fresh out of bed and, with a yawn, he assumed "the position". He was actually aiming pretty well when, midstream, he lifted both arms in the air and began *STRETCHING*! His head was now pointed toward the ceiling, leaving the stream to wander as it would with *EVERY* shift of his stretching body!

"Timmy!" I exclaimed, "Hang on to yourself! You have to *aim*!" I mean, *SERIOUSLY*, he didn't get the hands free model! Those cost *EXTRA*, and let's face it, kids are expensive enough! This experience was definitely shedding some light on the "smelly" subject. *Boys and their toys.* Although, I can't say all this was worse than the day I caught Bo, my two-year-old at the time, *DIPPING* his toothbrush *IN THE TOILET WATER* and then proceeding to brush his *TEETH*! *Eeeeewwwwww*!! I could see then that getting the boys to put the toilet seat up before they pee and then back down afterward was the *LEAST* of my worries.

A Petunia is a what?
By Jessica

The other day my two adorable boys were in the bathtub. I had to use the restroom so I plopped down onto the pot. My three-year-old, Ayden, looked at me and said, "No mom, not like that. You gotta stand up." (He thinks everyone has plumbing like him and his dad.)

"No, actually mommy doesn't have what you have," I replied. He stood up and tilted his head to try and get a BETTER look. I felt like an anatomy lesson!

"You don't have a Johnson, Mom?"

"No, baby," I chuckled.

"What do you have?" His little eyebrows furrowed and he just stood there waiting for an answer. I PANICKED! My husband and I didn't talk about what MINE would be called! Gosh, my husband has about TWELVE different names for his and I can't even come up with ONE for mine! I really didn't want my son walking through the grocery store one day, announcing that mommy has a VAGINA, and the words who-ha and va-jj just didn't seem appropriate for a three-year-old.

So, I looked at him and started to say something, then changed my mind about three times, and finally heard a word come out of my mouth. Ayden looked even more confused. And I thought back to what I had just told him...PETUNIA?...REALLY?? That is the BEST you can come up with?!? Yup, that's the word that I chose to describe the female anatomy. A flower. It didn't sound too bad until I thought about the fact that my mother-in-law is an expert GARDENER! She and Ayden plant new flowers every time she visits. I can only imagine the conversation between her and Ayden the day she decides to plant PETUNIAS! My poor kid will be even more confused! Oh well, what's a mom to do? I guess I will cross THAT bridge when we get there!

And the lesson we can learn from all this is...

By Jamie

It was weigh-in night once again for my little wrestler. When it comes to the sport of wrestling, getting your kid's weight is a necessity to be sure a 35-pound kid doesn't end up getting FLATTENED by a 95-pound kid. The night before the tournament, Michael planned to give Timmy and another teammate a ride to the weigh-in site, 'cause we figured there was no sense in all of us parents making the thirty-minute drive.

On his way out the door, I gave Michael directions to the teammate's house on Tucker Road. He questioned my certainty, *as if* I had trouble with directions *before*, and I said to him, "*I KNOW* what I am talking about! I have *personally* been to their house! I am the taxi service around here, ya know." (Insert hand on hip, eye roll, and some sass!) However, Michael was quite justified in his questioning of my directions because I *am* severely directionally challenged and have a habit of getting lost on the way to my own mailbox. My husband is a brave man, and against his better judgment, he embarked on his journey with my directions as his sole guide.

Meanwhile, Jess, Jake, and Mom stopped by for dinner so we could all hang out when Michael returned. As I was finishing up dinner, Jake found Michael's cell phone on the couch, and about 30 minutes later I received a call from a number I didn't recognize, only to hear Michael's voice on the other end. He couldn't find the house. At this time I was thinking, *Seriously, it is NOT that hard! There are only about FIVE houses on the whole road!* This was really odd to me because Michael *NEVER* gets lost. I told him I would call our friends and have them flash their porch lights to signal him. About 20 minutes later, our friends called me back saying there was *STILL* no sign of Michael. All of a sudden, I had this feeling that *Tucker* might *NOT* be the name of their road.

"Oh, no! *WHAT* is the name of your road?" I asked, hoping to hear the word "Tucker", knowing I wouldn't. Sure enough, I sent Michael to the *WRONG* road and he was *WITHOUT* his cell phone! *Oh-my-gosh!* My stomach just churned. How was I going to let Michael know he would *NEVER* find the right house?!? Our friend said he would go around the block and look for him and then just drive to the weigh-in himself before they closed. He assumed Michael probably gave up by now.

I was feeling *SOOOOO* bad. I had sent my husband on a *WILD* goose chase. Sad thing is, this *WASN'T* the first time! Unfortunately, there had been *MANY*. One in particular I can remember, was when Josh was three months old. He had a special twenty-dollar bottle that the doctor prescribed for me to use because he had trouble sucking.

One night after returning from a high school football game, I thought I left the bottle in the stands. So, *FREAKING OUT* about the twenty-dollar bottle, I had Michael drive back into town to retrieve it. He had to jump the fence, only to call me saying he couldn't find it. "Are you *sure* you didn't put it in the diaper bag?" he asked. "No, I am *SURE*," I said, as I went to double-check, and *THERE IT WAS*!

So, today, when I thought of my poor husband wandering a street *I* had sent him to *SO* confidently, I just wanted to cry! I felt so helpless and guilty; I just couldn't sit there and wait. Through glassy eyes, I looked at Jess, Jake, and Mom, and said I was going to look for him! I grabbed my keys and headed out the door.

Thinking back, I wonder *WHAT* I expected to accomplish. There was *NO* way he stayed on that same road for another half-hour. But *LOGIC* wasn't winning. I started my van, flung it into reverse, and backed up. Suddenly, I heard that *HORRIBLE* sound of metal hitting metal. *Oh, no!* I thought. *PLEASE tell me I did NOT just back into my sister's car!* (Ya see, backing into another vehicle is a sound I am, unfortunately, *VERY* familiar with. In the past ten years, I have backed into my sister's vehicle twice, my mom's once, and I also ran over someone's mail box backing out of their driveway. So, yeah, reverse is *NOT* my best direction. Michael says I need a bumper sticker that reads, *"Do Not Park Behind Me; You WILL Get Hit."*) Needless to say, I jumped out of my van and saw my sister's beautiful NEW red Traverse behind me! I didn't even go to check the damages; I just started crying and went back in the house!

I couldn't even talk. My family rushed to me, asking over and over again, "What's wrong?" My sister said jokingly, "What, did you hit my car?" Through my tears, I just nodded my head pathetically. "Oh, I'm kidding," she said, nonchalantly. "Really, what is *wrong* with you?" she asked.

My mom, picking up on the fact that *I* wasn't kidding, asked, "Did you really hit her car?" Still *SOBBING*, I nodded again.

"What, she is *SERIOUS*?!?" my sister said, in a panic. I just *SANK* onto the floor crying. I sent my husband to a *NON*-existent address, I *CRASHED* my sister's car, and I STILL didn't know where Michael was or when he would be home.

I told everyone to go home. I just wanted to climb in my bed and *SHUT DOWN*. Despite my protest, they stayed with me until Michael returned. He walked through the door, and with tear-stained cheeks I sheepishly looked at him. He said with his best Ricky Ricardo accent, "Luuuuucy! You got some splainin to do!"

It was after this comment that Jake, my brother-in-law, muttered behind a smile, "He doesn't know *HALF* the splainin she has to do!"

So, yeah, I "splained" everything to Michael. And, fortunately, the look he gave me was the one I see so often, and that is his loving, accepting grin, with an amused headshake. After 14 years of marriage, and all the shenanigans I put him through, he still looks at me like I am his world. I then informed him that the lesson we **ALL** could learn from today is, "Don't leave home without your cell phone!" (*Wink!*)

A challenge for you: "Gratitude Laughitude Attitude"

Life with kids can be exhausting, exasperating and totally chaotic at times. But in all the craziness, sometimes you just gotta laugh! I am truly thankful for this unpredictable, exhausting, entertaining and extremely fulfilling adventure. Today, I challenge you to make what I call, the "Fantastic Frustrations" list. I mean, sure, we all have those days when we walk into the kitchen and find cereal scattered all over the kitchen floor. Sure, we have to clean it up, and we may need to teach our kids boundaries or how to pour cereal, but the challenge we are faced with in the moment is to discover why we are actually thankful for such an experience, rather than letting it ruin our attitude and day.

Gratitude Laughitude Attitude Challenge:
Make a "Fantastic Frustrations" List.
Example: *I am so thankful that my kitchen looks like a box of cereal exploded in it because; this means I have adorable, self-sufficient kids!*

My Fantastic Frustrations:

1.

2.

3.

4.

PART 3

Mommalicious
From Baby Bump to Muffin Top and Rockin' It

Life with a new baby... it's so...beautiful??

By Jessica

Having a baby is a life changing experience...to put it *LIGHTLY*. When people think of new babies they often think of cuddly teddy bears, soft clean blankets, and glowing happy families, which was *exactly* what I imagined when *I* was pregnant. I had the whole fairytale, preconceived scenes playing in my head. Don't get me wrong, having a baby is definitely one of the most *magical* experiences ever, but one must also realize that along with the magic come a few moments not quite classified in the *"enchanting"* category. Accompanying those teddy bears and soft blankets are raging hormones, stretch marks, and *a whole lotta "up close and personal"* with my man. (Again, not the charming and enchanting *"up close and personal"* one would imagine!) Let me just tell ya some of the adjustments to my preconceived ideas about having a baby that I had to make.

Preconceived Scene #1 – Pack my favorite skinny jeans to wear home from the hospital. (Oh, and my makeup, to give me that extra-cute-mom look.)

I always *thought* I would be one of those *"in shape"* pregnant ladies. You know, the tiny figures that never have to wear maternity pants and have no extra fat anywhere else on their body, just a basketball out the front. Haha...*YEAH*...that was *NOT* me! FYI, upon meeting my husband I was 5'6" and in size six jeans. I loved the gym and thrived off shopping at health food stores. However, when I was pregnant I really took *"eating for two"* to the extreme. Two weeks before I delivered, I had gained 80 pounds and was stretching a size extra-large really, *really* thin. Had my mom not told me otherwise, I would have packed my size six jeans to wear home from the hospital. Yeah, *THAT* was a shocker to me! I figured once I popped the kid out I would *AT LEAST* go down a *couple* pants sizes. Nope, I squeezed my extra-large thighs back into my extra-large pants and they were *JUST* as snug as they were *BEFORE* having the baby.

Preconceived Scene #2 – My labor scene would be inspiring and adoring.

Aside from wearing maternity clothes out of the hospital, my hardest adjustment was changing from this young, perky, always put-together, and "wouldn't poop in front of her husband" type of person to having my husband in a front row seat to my brown starfish during the birth of our son. I had heard horror stories about women in labor pushing out a little more than a baby. I was praying and hoping that horror story wouldn't become my *REALITY*. I remember leaning over to Jake in the middle of pushing and asking, "Have I shit myself yet?" His face was so reassuring that I believed him when he responded, "No, baby. You're doing great!" Later on, I found out that *YES*, I *indeed* had pooped myself! I was *MORTIFIED*. All at once, my beautiful preconceived ideas came to a *screeching* halt. My vision of me holding my husband's hand through the contractions, never saying, "I hate you!"… having my cute little ponytail on top of my perspiring head (and not the nasty sweaty look, the "perfect movie" sweaty look, just to show how hard I was working)…and let's not forget the dramatic inspirational music with the perfect climaxes and lulls for effect. Yeah, the music stopped after finding out my husband *JUST* watched me basically take a shit. *Right in front of him.* **RIGHT in front of him***!!!*

Preconceived Scene #3 – Aglow with motherhood.

This is the scene where my body would return to its normal prebaby self and breastfeeding would give me the perfect plump breasts I had always wanted. The soft, warm glow of motherhood would surround me. I was, yet again, *SHOVED* back into reality! My body *DIDN'T* go back to normal. In fact, my belly button was looking so depressed I was beginning to think it would never return to its happy, whistling self. And my breasts! Well, *PLUMP* is an *understatement*. They felt like water balloons that had been filled *WAY* beyond what they were ever meant to hold and seemed to explode every time the baby cried, leaving me with puddles of breast milk down the front of my shirt. And warm mom glow? The only glow I had was from my glistening locks that hadn't seen shampoo in three days!

Preconceived Scene #4 – Pooping myself during labor is the WORST my hubby will see.

Another, *NOT*-so-picture-perfect moment was the issue of learning how to use the bathroom again. Every woman who has been through labor knows there is a fine art to keeping things clean after having a baby. It takes a delicate touch to get the job done without ripping out the six stitches now holding her lady parts together. About three days after being home, I had used the bathroom and noticed I had some stripes left in my white panties. *TOTALLY* embarrassed, I shoved them to the bottom of the laundry basket deep enough so my husband wouldn't see them. I figured I would take care of them later with the pre-spot, and I sat down to read a book for some quiet time while my little one slept. Moments later, my husband walked in and began changing for his golf game. He charged into our closet and came out empty-handed, asking me if I had seen his favorite golf shirt. "Nope," I said, not taking my eyes off my book. He went back into our closet and I heard him start rummaging through our laundry basket. I felt my breathing stop and my pulse begin to race! *ALL* I could think about was my underwear I had tried to hide! He came out of the closet with a smirk on his face. "Holy racing stripes, babe!" As if *THAT* wasn't *ENOUGH*, he went on to say, "I mean, those are NASCAR size." Really? I mean *really*? I'm gonna say that one more time...***REALLY***? Can I feel any *LESS* sexy?!?

Yes, my preconceived scenes changed as I experienced them in real life. But I will say this: although my belly was hanging over my jeans like a flat tire, and my hair needed to see some serious product, or even just a brush, and my husband had seen a side of me I swore *NEVER* to show him, there actually was a sweet glow around my new family, and that was the glow of *LOVE*. My husband had seen me at what I thought to be my worst and loved me even more. I felt even closer to him. One day, as we sat on our bed just staring at this brand new being, I realized my *REALITY* was even *MORE* magical than I had imagined.

Who said?!?

By Jamie

Who got to sit in their big giant chair and decide what is *ACCEPTABLE* and what is *NOT*? What is cool and what is un-cool? Who said pimples and braces aren't the bomb? Seriously, braces cost as much as a wardrobe of designer clothes! That should count for something, right? (Perhaps Abercrombie should put out a line of the most expensive braces around.) Who said women should have smooth legs, but if a man doesn't have enough hair on his legs then he's not man enough? *SERIOUSLY*, who got to make such important life-impacting decisions, 'cause I would like to give the person who invented *STARCH* a piece of my mind!

Michael grabbed out a shirt to wear the other night and it was *WRIN-KLY*. Ya see, I gave up ironing over a decade ago when my first kid was born. (Lol! Don'tcha just love how I say, "I *GAVE* it up"? It almost sounds heroic. Like, "Um, yeah, when my son was born I decided to give up my *WILD* side and settle down.") Yeah, so as I was saying, I *heroically* gave up ironing the day Josh was born so I could lovingly devote my time to him. (Yup, I'm gonna stick with that version. It sounds better.)

The question we need to be asking is, "How come wrinkled isn't the "in" style?" Some shirts actually *COME* pre-wrinkled! I love them. I can wad them up, throw them in a suitcase and pull them out the next day, freshly wrinkled and ready to go. So I have to ask, why aren't wrinkled work shirts or wrinkled polo shirts *JUST* as acceptable? It's *SO* annoying. If you buy it wrinkled you can't wear it pressed, but if you buy it pressed you can't wear it wrinkled. Seriously, if the *FIRST* person didn't decide to *IRON* we would all have perfectly acceptable clothing.

With my *INGENIOUS* mind, I've figured out a way to beat the system and *obey* the ridiculous rule of not having wrinkly clothes *without* actually ever having to iron. My method is to put all my "can't-be-wrinklies" in the same load. Then I hang them up as *SOON* as they finish drying and are still a bit warm. If I don't get to the dryer quick enough to get that "ironed-ish" look, I just toss the really bad ones back in the washer, hoping to do better next time. Lol!

I think I might just rebel against whoever got to make all of those decisions about what is *COOL* and decide to start a new "wrinkly everything" trend; it would be so much easier. First, it's *NO IRONING*. Next, maybe I will quit shaving my legs. The possibilities are *ENDLESS*!

Are you prego??
By Jessica

It was Sunday morning and I was getting dressed for church. Unlike those "after baby" days where you can get away with going to church in your frumpy clothes and hiding in the back, I figured I better dress nice because I was on the worship schedule this morning. I looked in the mirror and noticed my "after baby" belly was becoming a little more pronounced than usual. *Hmmm...I was under the impression that this left-over belly was supposed to continue shrinking, not expand outward again.* Granted, I had put on a little gray dress with an empire waist, and if you don't have a perfectly flat tummy when wearing that particular style it's as if you just hung a sign on yourself that says, "Look at my belly!" But it made me feel cuter and skinnier than the sweats I'd been wearing all week, so out the door me and my *NOT*-so-empire waist went.

Later that very morning, after I finished leading worship for our church, one of the elderly ladies stopped me and said, "Oh, Sweetie, I couldn't even tell you were pregnant when you were up there on that stage. But now I can see your little baby bump. You are just so adorable." *OH, MY GOSH! You look pregnant, Jess! You really need to do something with yourself*, I screamed in my head as I smiled at the lady and then rushed to find my seat.

During the sermon, I tried to keep my mind on our Pastor's message and not brainstorm about what *gym* I was going to join as soon as church ended. *Heck, maybe I should go do some crunches in the prayer room before I have to sing the closing song of the service!*

Finally, church ended, and I was quickly saying my goodbyes and making my way to the door when yet another woman approached me and said, "Hey, Jess, myself and a couple of other ladies were taking bets as to whether or not you are expecting baby number three. So, are you? You know...pregnant?" In that moment I had the choice to say, "Nope, not pregnant! Who's the lucky winner?!?" or to simply go home and put a pillow over my head. I stood there, knowing my only obvious choice was to be nice and pretend that she didn't just call me *FAT!* I politely laughed and said, "Nope...not pregnant..just chubby," adding a *wink*! I'm pretty sure I *died* a little that day. I got home and thought I might feel better if I took some prenatal vitamins.

Later that evening, I went over to my sister's. "Wow, are you pregnant?

> If you come home with the same kids you left with, it's a good day.

You look like you're glowing." Her words were like nails on a chalkboard. Oh, yeah! There is a GLOW all right! I thought. *A glow from the FIRE that was brewing in me to KNOCK OUT the next idiot that decided to ask a mother of a nine-month-old if SHE WAS PREGNANT!* Needless to say, my sister kept her head that night and I went home and watched Beachbody paid programming while eating a bowl of chocolate chip cookie dough.

Naturally, after my binge, the next day I made a commitment with a friend to be fitness buddies. I was rather excited! I knew she would be a motivating fitness pal. A twenty-minute workout three times a week sounded easy enough, but the next thing I knew she was texting me every day about how many miles she had run. *EVERY DAY! WOW!!!!* I was lucky if I got up off the couch during naptime to go to the bathroom on my *non-workout* days. Never mind working out *EXTRA* or even *MORE* than my twenty minutes on my *workout* days!

Okay, I obviously signed myself up with a real go-getter! So I *TRIED* getting my butt in gear and began counting calories from this website she recommended. I thought it was great! The first day I signed up I happened to be so busy that I had no time to eat, so I was under for my calorie intake by the time I went to bed. I was *GEEKED*!!! I told myself, *This is going to be easy!* Well, Day 2 rolled around. It was a mundane day, and I had time to consume all three meals, and yet I found myself a little hungry after dinner. So, I got on the website to check my calorie intake and found I only had about 30 to spare. Yeah...that's an *APPLE*. Don't get me wrong, I love my fruit, but I wanted something with a *LITTLE* more substance. Seeing that I couldn't find anything under 30 calories, I went to bed not only hungry, but *GRUMPY*.

On Day 3, I woke up hearing, *Mayday! Mayday! Must have food!* in my head and I knew today would be rough. And it *WAS*. But while I listened to my stomach grumble and began to think the dog food looked appetizing, I realized something. For three days I did *NOTHING* but think about food! What I *COULD* and *COULDN'T* eat. It's like when you are posing for a picture and are supposed to hold still, your nose itches. I became grouchy with my kids and my husband. I also realized that while my mind was so preoccupied I wasn't enjoying the little moments that were right in front of me. Like the fact that my youngest was *ACTUALLY* getting along with his brother, or that my oldest was reading his books in his room. I was missing out on playing chase and shooting dart guns, or making Mr. Potato Heads!

Now don't get me wrong, I am a huge advocate for a healthy diet and exercise. All I am saying is when we get so driven to be something different than what we *ARE*, we should probably evaluate the motives behind it. My motive was getting into those pre-baby jeans. *WHO SAID* I have to get back into those things anyway? In *MY* opinion we should go shopping for a new wardrobe after each kid! I am *not* overweight by any means. Could I stand to tone and work out? *Absolutely*! But I will do it when I can, and in the meantime I'm *NOT* going to worry about what Susie looks like and the fact that her baby is six months younger than mine. I am going to *SOAK* up my cute little monsters and all of their adorable stages they go through! I can worry about being in shape *LATER*, when I'm 90 (*wink*!). Life is so short. I don't want to look back and wonder why I wasted time missing magical moments with my kids to be a size smaller. So *WHAT* that I have a muffin top around my middle?! I would rather be chunky and dive into my kids' lives than be a size six and miss everything! Why do we have kids? To spend *TIME* with them and truly enjoy them before they grow up and live their own lives! And *THAT* is what I aim to do!

Young and Perky

By Jessica

Not long ago, Jake and I had plans to meet up with friends for a play date, and let me tell ya, before we left home I was *DREADING* it. One of the wives who would be there was "Barbie". (Ya know, *beautiful* and a size six...basically the "whole package". One of those women I *DON'T* really want to stand next to after I just popped out a kid. A woman who would *probably* only spend five minutes on her hair and wardrobe and would *STILL* look better than I did, even though I tried on seven different shirts and spent *AT LEAST 30 MINUTES* creating this mess on top of my head.)

On the car ride over, I was thinking out loud to my husband and wondering how it would feel to be so *perfect.* "I wonder if she feels incredible about herself. Or maybe she still has all the same demons I have." *Gosh,* my mind trailed, *are we FOREVER trying to get rid of those demons...do we fight the "appearance demon" all our lives? For REAL, as women, how MUCH time do we spend thinking about how we LOOK??? How much time do we spend comparing ourselves to everyone else, NEVER feeling good enough?* I wondered how we would feel about ourselves if we just didn't put so much of our value on our appearance. *What if we simply looked at ourselves and recognized that we are all diverse and pregnancy affects us ALL differently? I know it's cliché, but really, WHAT IF we just ACCEPTED ourselves?!? How much more FUN would we have?!?*

But I wasn't done being stuck in my negative mindset. I proceeded to tell my husband that I was looking at our honeymoon pictures earlier that week. "What happened to me, baby?" I asked him with sincerity. Only three years ago...and yet, I was amazed at how young and vibrant I looked in the photos. I was so *skinny* and *beautiful.* No dark circles under my eyes, no love handles jiggling with every step I took. I even had a *glow*! My husband responded, "You are still beautiful, Sweetie." I had to smile...for a second, at least. *THEN,* being a *WOMAN,* I kept arguing, letting those demons continue to rob even more of my time. "Yeah, but I was so *VIBRANT.* I seemed so *ALIVE,*" I said. And then it came to me, *Maybe that was because I was having the hottest sex ever, every night. After all, it WAS my honeymoon.* (Nowadays, I feel like if I make it to the finish line without falling asleep or a kid interrupting, it was a hot *enough* night.) And now when I look in the mirror after I wake up, I see black circles, dry skin, and a drool trail running down my jaw line. Not so sexy any more.

My husband obviously went off into his own dreamland, as told by his face. "Yeah, you *WERE* young and perky," was what floated out of his mouth and *FELL* like a *HUNDRED POUND WEIGHT* in my *LAP.*

(Hmmm...yeah, not *quite* the support I was looking for.) He tried to bounce back with, "We have *BOTH* changed."

I looked at him and laughed. "You haven't changed a bit!" (My husband has gained and lost ten pounds throughout our three year marriage. Whoop-dee-doo. I, on the other hand, have changed *A LOT* with each pregnancy. I mean 85-POUNDS-*A-LOT*! And even though we are done having kids I am still 35 pounds heavier than I'd *LIKE* to be.)

I sat there wishing I looked like I did on my honeymoon, and then a *HUGE* revelation smacked me in the face. Even in my *SKINNY* days... wearing that little black bikini, tight-fitting shirts and jeans, I was STILL telling myself I had to work out *MORE* and *EAT LESS* to be *SKINNIER*! Realizing this, I began to dream of the day I would be able to accept myself. My date with "Barbie" was going to make accepting myself that much harder to do *TODAY*, but I knew I wanted to simply be in awe that my body could have two beautiful children. Some people are *never* gifted that opportunity. The *LEAST* I could do is be thankful and grateful for it! The cycle will *NEVER* end until I change my perspective. I *AM* thankful I can have children! I am *grateful* God blessed me with two beautiful boys!! And *THAT* needs to be my focus!

Nice Headlights!!
By Jessica

"Oh what a day!" I uttered to my husband, as I plopped myself down in the chair across from him. As I verbally unloaded all my cares of the day to Jake, I began the process of nursing my baby boy to sleep. (Before I go on, I guess I should inform you that sex is almost obsolete in our marriage right now. Having a two-year-old and a three-month-old has basically drained me of all energy. *ALL* energy. In fact, I just told myself it was time to clean the toilet before someone comes over and is grossed out by the science project currently multiplying in the bowl. I know a toilet, by nature, is gross, but I am *pretty* sure it isn't supposed to take on the characteristics of a Petri dish. Seeing that

I am only getting about three dispersed hours of sleep a night, cleaning the house is *NOT* at the top of my list. I am just happy if I change my two-year-old's diaper before it falls to his ankles!)

Anyway, back to nursing Zayne while I tell Jake my woes of the day. I was *SO* engrossed in telling my story, I didn't realize that the flap on my nursing bra was hanging open with no baby attached. Apparently, I forgot to refasten it when I put Zayne on the other breast. So there I sat, with Zayne's one-eyed friend staring at my husband, obviously beckoning him. I kept going on and on, and then noticed my husband drop his gaze from my eyes down to my chest a couple times. All I could think was, *Wow, he's really checking out the goods!* I continued talking, and finally he shook his head and said, "I'm sorry, babe, but I can't concentrate with your boob hanging out. I can't think about anything, but seeing **both** of them." Needless to say, I was *flattered*. (There is a sweet time after a baby is born, when your husband becomes *SO* desperate for sex, that he will start cleaning, giving compliments, and become the adorable person he was when you were dating.) I think I was just excited that he didn't seem to notice the red and purple stretch marks that crossed my breast like dry, cracked sand that hadn't seen water in years, or the fact that my hair was greasy from the lack of showers.

During these days, I feel more like a cow supplying the milk than a *HOT* wife. But in that moment, my husband couldn't take his eyes off my "milk makers". He just *WANTED* me! In that moment he did not see the worn-out mom who had merely forgotten to fasten the nursing bra. Well, maybe he did, but in his sexually-deprived state, this worn-out momma was looking *pretty darn HOT*. Either way he made me feel like the woman of his dreams, and I *NEEDED* that.

A challenge for you: "Proud To Be Me"

Oh yes! Body image, ya gotta love that chapter. (Lol!) You can probably guess what the challenge is today. Yup! It's a challenge to talk nice about your BODY! This challenge is extremely important. The way we perceive ourselves and the way we talk about ourselves, affects us both emotionally and physically. If you will commit to this challenge for one week, your countenance and energy will transform. Similar to the PMS challenge, it is time to get in touch with your "Awesomeness" *again*.

Now, for those of you who do not feel worthy of such an exercise, let me ask you this. If you noticed your daughter being emotionally harmful to herself, by constantly putting herself down, how would you feel? Of course, as moms we would never want our daughters to say half the stuff to themselves, that we say to ourselves. Well, guess what! Starting at a very early age, those adorable little girls hear us chit-chat with our friends about our so-called frizzy hair, poor complexion, and undesired muffin tops. All too soon, they adopt the "lingo" as their own. Our kids learn by *example*! Remember that saying that goes, "Do as I say, not as I do"? Yeah, we all know how effective that is...just look how well it worked for us. lol

I truly, hope you commit to this challenge and genuinely choose to be nice to yourself. *You are worth it*!

Proud To Be Me Challenge:

Name 7 ways your body is Awesome. Then, **EVERYDAY**, read and **BELIEVE** what you have written! If you can't think of anything nice to say... ask your kids or a close friend...and then choose to **BELIEVE THEM**.

Example: I have beautiful eyes. I am healthy. My body has the ability to repair itself. I have a warm smile. My curves make great cushions for snuggling and pillows for my kids during story time.
The possibilities are endless!!!

"Proud To Be Me"
My Body is awesome because...

1. _____

2. _____

3. _____

4. _____

5. _____

6. _____

7. _____

PART 4

I Need Chocolate...STAT
It's Just Been One of Those Days

When they are laughing together... sometimes we should worry!

By Jamie

When a mom hears her toddlers laughing and playing together, two emotions are triggered. First, she feels all warm and fuzzy 'cause the two toddlers she just pulled off each other as if they were in a death match are now BFFs. The second emotion is PANIC. *Oh great, what trouble are they getting into NOW?* All parents learn that when the laughter continues and continues, without an argument, *TROUBLE* is in the air. Let me just tell ya a couple of my own "laughable" experiences.

2 SISTERS' MISGUIDED MANUAL TO MOTHERHOOD

One morning, in attempts to be productive, my *ingenious* mom-mind thought to give my toddlers a pen and paper to play "office" while I sat at the computer "playing" office myself. Oh, and it WORKED!! NO ONE was in my lap trying to push buttons, or pulling on my shirt to tattle on the other, or even asking me to do something for them. As I typed away, they were working and even giggling together. *Wow, this worked out better than I imagined.* My gloating thoughts were interrupted when I heard Josh say to Kate, "Ok, now let's do your feet." *Hmmmmm. A three-year-old with a pen saying "let's do your feet."* I couldn't spin my office chair around FAST enough! Sure enough, Kate was obviously Josh's canvas. There was red ink all over her belly and down her legs and Josh was getting ready to make her feet match the rest of his work. The artist himself, was RADIATING with pride. And although I knew it was a priceless piece, I had to take the pen away and *draw* a bath.

Sometime after the "Picasso" incident, the giggling came from the toy room upstairs. It was the type of laughter that SURELY was inspired by illegal entertainment, so I went RUNNING! As I headed up the stairs, I could hear running water, and when I rounded the corner, I saw Josh standing on a stool filling up a toy coffee pot from their Little Tykes Kitchen. I then followed the trail of water OUT of the bathroom, DOWN the hall, and ACROSS the toy room floor leading to Kate, who was having just a good 'ole time "washing the dishes" in their Little Tykes kitchen sink! They were having a blast, and I was trying to find the silver lining in water *everywhere*. After all, the floors WERE overdue for a good scrubbing; maybe they would find scrub brushes just as fun. My fantasies of illegal child labor melted away when they poured me a cup of "coffee". *Who knows, maybe all this*

Must have coffee!! It's 5am somewhere!

enthusiasm will last through their teen years? (Hahahahaha! Now *I'm* the one giggling!)

Speaking of "giggling", another incident *DEFINITELY* worth mentioning took place in the grocery store. Both of the kids were sitting in the basket of the cart, playing what seemed to be quite an amusing game of "make believe". Taking advantage of their content confinement, I raced through the store, piling my items in the "kid holder" part of the cart. After all, I only needed a *few* things. Eventually, I couldn't even *SEE* the kids for all the stuff I had managed to pile into such a small space. The kids were laughing and playing (seriously, how often does *THAT* happen?), so I took a moment to just b-r-o-w-s-e. Eventually, the giggling became so constant I had to see for myself what was so funny. I wasn't expecting any trouble. I mean they were caged in the back of a shopping cart, what *TROUBLE* could there *BE*? I peered over the pile of items to see my precious munchkins *SPLATTERED* in *GREEN PAINT!* What!?! For real?!? Josh had swiped a bottle of craft paint and used his ingenious three-year-old kid mitts to break the seal, unscrew the cap, and have a creative art session with his sister!

Resisting the urge to walk away and pretend they were someone *ELSE'S* kids, there I stood in the fabric aisle, holding a saturated bottle of paint in one hand and all four of the *green* mitts in my other. A Store associate came upon the scene (the very *embarrassing* scene), and with wide eyes she grabbed the opened container and handed me some old fabric. I frantically wiped up the kids while thinking of a plan to change my hair color and name just to be able to shop there again! Just when I thought it couldn't get any more embarrassing, those famous words came over the loud speaker and echoed off *EVERY* wall. "Clean up in fabrics!" Those words are *MUCH* funnier when heard on a movie that I am watching, while thinking the whole time, *Ha, that wouldn't happen in real life.* Well, it was happening in *MY* real life!

After the grand announcement, three more associates joined our little paint party. *Oh great, three more witnesses that will be able to place ME at the scene of the crime.* One began spraying the floor under my cart, and I noticed the other two just shaking their heads as they stared down the aisle I previously visited. This would have been a good time to grab my cart and *RUN*, but nope, I had to see *EXACTLY* what was attracting such a look. *OH*, my *GOSH*! There was a steady line of green paint down the *ENTIRE* aisle. *Hmmmmmm?* I gave the associate a puzzled glance as if to say, "There is no way *WE* did all that." I glanced over to my green monsters in the cart, then back to the associate, and desperately said, "Could you tell me what aisle the chocolate is in?...And I mean the *HARD* stuff!"

Can I just get a license?
By Jessica

Why is it that my kids save their *CRAZIEST* behavior for the times when I *MOST* need them to help me convince strangers that I am an awesome mom who has it *ALL* together? I mean, seriously! I want people to have warm fuzzies from seeing my adorable, well-behaved children, not having contraceptives be at the forefront of their mind as we walk out the door. But recently I lost my license and hadn't a clue of how to get a new one, so I did what any busy mom would do: I *DIDN'T* research it and simply went to the Secretary of State, figuring *THEY* could tell me what needed to be done. I'd sign some form and walk out feeling productive and, not to mention, legal to drive.

When I walked into the Secretary of State with my two little towheads, I took a number and was *DELIGHTED* to see we were only behind three people. For real, those lines can be endlessly long at times, but this would be a *PIECE OF CAKE*! My boys were already doing great. They just sat in their seats playing with their toy cars. *Sweet!* But then they called my number and the clerk asked me for *THREE* different forms of identification. I *PANICKED!* This is where the research would have come in handy.

Most people might have given up at this point, but, thankfully, it had been *MONTHS* since I cleaned out my diaper bag/mom-purse; *CERTAINLY* there would be some old junk mail taking up space, right? I began digging, trying to find *SOMETHING* with my name on it, while the clerk peered at me over her half-moon glasses with an irritated gaze. I'm fairly sure she even gave her co-worker the "We have one of *those* Moms" expression. Lost in the depths of my oversized mom bag, I didn't notice Zayne climbing over a half-wall that led into the back of the office until it was almost too late to retrieve him! Not wanting to face THAT embarrassment, I *BOLTED* over and grabbed him, saying, "Buddy, no, no. Ayden, watch your brother for two minutes."

With my four-year-old babysitting my two-year-old (such a great plan, right?), I confidently continued excavating through my purse, pretending *NOT* to be fully aware of all the impatient eyes on me. I wasn't ready to give up, yet, because I had *ALREADY* managed to find an insurance card and a SAM'S membership card. (Sometimes *NEVER* cleaning out your mom purse *REALLY* pays off!) *Just ONE more thing!* I glanced toward my boys again, and there was two-year-old Zayne, sitting on the floor kicking off his boots, *NOT* accompanied by his "babysitter". Frantically craning my neck to find Ayden, I spotted my four-year-old drawing circles *ON THE WALL* with an *INK PEN!!!* *WHAT??????* I grabbed Zayne up off the floor and carried him back to the counter, all the while giving Ayden

"The Look", to which he responded, "What mom?" with a smirk and a shrug of his not-so-innocent little shoulders. To my relief, Ayden put the pen down and dutifully walked over to my side. Goodness knows what the clerk was thinking at this moment, but fortunately she didn't boot me aside and call the next number.

Still not one to give up easily, I basically held Zayne in some sort of Nazi-Ninja hold as he struggled to grab *EVERYTHING* on the counter, while I dove into my purse once again and *FINALLY* found a plane ticket from Denver with my name on it!!! (I honestly think the clerk would have given me a new license to simply get me out of her hair at this point.) While I signed the paperwork, Zayne was reeling in my arms, trying to get free.

The lovely clerk gave me a sour look and said, "Ok, now you *DO* realize we have to take your picture, right?"

As I tried to make eye contact with her through my son's flying white curls in the midst of his tantrum, I answered, "Yes....right...a picture. You can't just use the *OLD* one?" By her piercing look I figured out *THAT* was a *DUMB* question. "Okay, let's do the picture!" I tried to sound like a mom who had EVERYTHING under control, but let's face it; at this point, the *ONLY* person who would buy the act would be *ME*.

I walked over to the white wall and stood on the X. Still worried about what else my four-year-old might get into, I peeked over at Ayden, who was lying face down on the not-so-clean (okay, it was *NASTY!*) carpet. Thoughts of sanitizing his face with my hand gel flashed through my mind. I attempted to smile for the picture while holding Zayne between my legs as he still threw his fit, and I prayed the picture *WOULDN'T* reflect my mood. *Finally DONE! I can get these boys OUTTA HERE!*

Of course, while we are walking back to the car, they amazingly turned back into my sweet little boys. Zayne held my hand without protest, and Ayden was holding Zayne's other hand, being a great big brother. By the time we got back to the car, they were *SUCH DARLINGS* that it looked like I had given them a happy pill! No arguing while getting into their car seats. No screaming on the way home. *COMPLETE ANGELS. If only "Miss Half-Moon Glasses" could have seen this side of them. Then she'd know what a fantastic mom I am! (Wink!)*

Don'tcha just LOVE a day at the doctor's office?!

By Jamie

Don'tcha just *LOVE* carting your kids to the doctor's office? Yeah, *NOT* really. It's nothing personal against the doctors, themselves; I am actually extremely grateful for their knowledge and ability to help my kids be healthy. But I *REALLY* avoid doctor appointments like I avoid the plague, unless of course we *HAVE* the plague (Lol!).

Don'tcha just love it when they ask you to come a few minutes early to fill out paperwork? *What! Early?!? Lady, are you kidding me? I* have a two-year-old and a three-and-a-half-year-old! I will be LUCKY if I make it there on time or even AT ALL. That's if the men in white coats don't snatch me up before I get everyone into the van! But of course I always politely responded, "Okay. No problem." *Ha!*

And you definitely gotta think the paperwork is a blast! Yup, re-writing your address eighteen times as if it was a punishment from a teacher (Lol!). Remember those days.....*I will not talk in class...I will not talk in class.* About halfway through the paperwork you're thinking, *Hmmm, if only there was some machine that would copy and paste my address as many times as needed.*

Once you are finished with the paperwork all that's left is the 45-minute wait to see the doctor, which naturally leaves you wondering, *Why did I work so hard to be "early"?* Forty-five minutes in a room with magazines to dump, diaper bags to explore, germ infested toys, and germ infested kids. *Oh, please, can we just stay here all day?!?*

But really, the best part is waiting in the six-by-six exam room. There's nothing like trying to keep an energetic young boy happy and tame in such a small "cage" with all kinds of "don't touch"-ables! The words, "Stop pushing the buttons on the automatic table!", "Don't touch the scopes!", "Don't turn the water on!", and "No, you don't need a three-foot Q-tip right now!" seem to *ECHO* off the walls.

Oh, yeah, and ya gotta love that spinny chair, *ESPECIALLY* if you have more than one kid in the room. The range of games they come up with! My favorite is, "Hey, let's see how fast we can spin you until you fly off and crash into the wall." When the doctor catches us, I usually get the stink-eye. But, hey, I figure they are entertained (the doctor hasn't had to spend the last 30 minutes in this "shoebox" with them), and if they happen to get a gash that requires stitches, we are *AT LEAST* in the right place! Right?!?

Oh, and that strip of paper on the table. Whew! Thank goodness they put that there so we don't spread our germs (*sarcasm* implied). Nope, that strip of paper just invokes a whole new set of phrases to repeat, like, "Stop *PLAYING* with the paper!", "Don't *LICK* the paper!", and "Don't sit *UNDER* the paper!" Usually by the time the doctor walks in, the paper is torn into at least four pieces and scattered on the floor. But, hey, I am just happy I got my kid to quit playing with the "hazardous trash" receptacle.

Ya know what I *REALLY* would love?!? How about when we have to visit the doctor's, we pile the kids in a holding room with magazines to rip up and diaper bags to dump out, while in a separate waiting area the moms enjoy a cup of coffee and a warm, moist towelette. Yeah, that *PROBABLY* wouldn't be covered by insurance. (*Wink*!)

Knock, Knock...Housekeeping...
By Jamie

Aren't vacations great?! Warm days in the sun, lying by the pool just sipping a cold beverage, not a care in the world. That is until you vacation with *toddlers*. Then it's more like chasing scattered bouncy balls in the sun. While at the pool you keep such a close eye on them you dare not even blink, and everywhere you go you keep obsessively counting them just to be sure you return with the same number of kids you left with. *Returning home a kid short might be tough to explain to the grandparents.*

By the end of one vacation, in particular, I remember having *SERIOUS* doubts about whether or not I should be responsible for a kid. I thought perhaps I should have just gotten a puppy. At least I could put a puppy on a leash or even tie it up to keep it from running away! *NOPE*, never got a puppy. At the *WISE* old age of nineteen, I unexpectedly dove into parenthood headfirst. And when Josh was three and Kate was two, we took our first family vacation to Orlando, Florida.

> Do laundry TODAY!!! The kids are all out of underwear.

The day after our arrival, Michael and I thought it would be fun to tour Downtown Disney. Michael got the kids dressed and I, of course, was running back and forth grabbing diapers, wipes, water, juice boxes, and *EVERYTHING* under the sun, so it seemed. But, hey, we were under the Florida sun, so I wasn't complaining.

As usual, Michael and the kids were ready before I was, and the kids were passing the time by running out on the hall balcony and back into the hotel room. Michael was standing with the door open and they were laughing as they went in and out, over and over again. Finally, I went to the bedroom to grab *ONE* last item and on my way out I bumped into Michael, who was coming to hurry me along. When we returned, Josh stood there in the doorway...**alone.** I began to *PANIC*! "Where is Kate?" I said, as I felt my pulse begin to race.

"She went in the elevator," he responded so nonchalantly. This was only a four floor complex and we were right next to the elevator, but *STILL, this was my BABY.* Michael took off for the stairs and I peered over the balcony, keeping a steady eye on the elevator doors. When those doors slid open, little "Dorothy" knew she was not in Kansas anymore! I could not see her, but I could hear her loud cry "Mommy!" Just seconds later Michael had her in his arms. When he returned her safely to me, I said, "Let's not do that again. I really *WOULD* like to return home with two children." I then added sarcastically, "Maybe one less *husband*, but *DEFINITELY* two children."

Somehow we managed to make it through the next four days without too many casualties. We suffered a couple scraped knees and lost a few scoops of ice cream to gravity, but each evening we tucked two adorable and exhausted children into bed. By the last day of our vacation, we were proud and worn-out parents, and all we had left on our to-do list was to sleep in!!! Apparently Josh didn't get the memo, because he was tapping on my forehead *pretty* early the next morning. I tried to stall him with a movie, but he kept waking me up to tell me what was happening every sixty seconds. Once it became perfectly clear that sleep was *NOT* an option for me, I took Josh to the pool so I could *AT LEAST* enjoy the sun.

When Michael and Kate finally joined us, I asked him what time Kate had woken up. "I'm not sure," he said. Seeing the puzzled look on my face, he went on to explain that he was woken up by a knock at the front door.

"Who's there?" he answered, rushing to wrap a towel around his waist.

"Housekeeping."

"I am still in here; we don't need our room cleaned," he said frantically, hoping to avoid the awkward moment of the housekeeping lady catching him wrapped in a towel that didn't seem to fit *ALL* the way around his waist. As he was telling me the story, I was amused at his predicament and even began to giggle, but I couldn't help but wonder *HOW* the housekeeping lady had *ANYTHING* to do with what time Kate woke up.

"Is this your little girl out here?" the lady said through the closed door. By now my eyebrows began to furrow, and the pieces of the story were connecting in a way I wasn't sure I liked.

"No," he said. "Our little girl is still sleeping in her bed."

"Well, she says this is her room." So, still in his towel, Michael cracked the door and, sure enough, the big blue eyes peering up at him were Kate's.

"Hi, Daddy," she said, so innocently. *What!!!* My thoughts overtook Michael and his story. *My daughter left the room!?! I mean, SERIOUSLY, what kind of parents have their child returned to them by HOUSEKEEP-ING???...while they are at the pool and sleeping!!!!!!* Yup! *Shoulda just gotta puppy!* Once my mind stopped racing and conjuring up a way to implant a GPS device into my children's wrists, I just had to thank God for His protection and honest people.

Despite the fact that we lost our daughter *twice*, we *DID* return from vacation with the same number of kids we left with. And what's more impressive is they were also the originals—no replacements. So, all in all, our first family vacation was a success. Maybe *SOMEDAY* down the road I will be able to lie by the pool with my eyes shut. Until then, I am thankful for the stressful fun that accompanies my *adorable* little toddlers.

A day out is so refreshing...RIGHT?

By Jamie

Oh, YAY! I hung up the phone and began the "rushing whirlwind" ritual that this occasion always calls for, running all over the house like a freight train that has jumped its tracks. I needed to get the kids dressed, pack the diaper bag, change out of my *oh-so-comfy* sweat pants, and get everything and everybody loaded into the truck, 'cause this momma was going *OUT!* Simple, *RIGHT?*

It seems rushing around is unavoidable whenever we leave the house. Ya see, there never seems to be *ENOUGH* time. One would assume that an hour would be plenty of time to get everyone dressed and packed up. But, what I sometimes forget to account for is someone pooping in their diaper on the way *OUT* the door, or my toddler *SPILLING* his cup of milk all over the table and onto the floor. And it especially slows me down when the baby refuses to leave my hip, and I must practice my one-armed make-up application skills. The list of things that *CAN* and *DO* happen goes on and on. Just when I think I have outsmarted "Murphy" and his annoying "law" by giving myself an extra half-hour for those spilt milk delays, something *CRAZIER* happens, devouring my cushion of time and driving me into a rushing whirlwind once again. No matter how quickly I manage to buckle everyone into their seats, we can't actually leave the driveway without running back into the house *at least once* to grab a forgotten item or two, or three...or *SEVEN*.

    Despite *ALL* that, this particular day I decided that, no matter how long this ritual took, we were going *OUT!* Out of the house. The kids and I were looking forward to joining some other moms and their kids at the mall. I was excited and anticipated the fun adventure ahead. (Oh, my gosh! Was it *EVER* an adventure!)

    On my way to the mall, I stopped at my cousin's house to borrow her double stroller. It was my first time to the mall with two kids, and I thought the stroller would prevent me from looking like a sideshow. (Yeah, I have since realized that my life *IS* a sideshow, and if I could *CHARGE* for all the entertainment my family continues to provide, well, my hubby could retire. Lol!)

    When I arrived at the mall, I realized I was 15 minutes late for our meet-up time, so once again the "rushing whirlwind" began. I lugged the big, clunky double stroller out of the truck and did my best to remember how my cousin said to open the snazzy contraption. Finally, I plopped my two-year-old, Josh, into his seat, and then grabbed my nine-month-old daughter, Kate, out of her car seat. Just as I was about to set her in the stroller, it totally *COLLAPSED!* I looked down, and *THERE* was Josh, folded in the stroller with only his head and arms sticking out. He wasn't hurt, but he wasn't very *HAPPY* with the situation either! Meanwhile, it had started raining. *Of course, Murphy!* In my panic to free my son and avoid the condescending stares of anyone in the parking lot who might see us and think me *LESS* than a *COMPLETELY* competent mother, I sat my daughter down next to the stroller on the wet pavement. Once I unfolded Josh and pulled him out, I sat him next to Kate and then tried to figure out how to latch the stroller, because whatever I did the *FIRST* time *OBVIOUSLY* didn't work! After a few attempts, I finally latched the dang thing. At last, wet butts and all, they were both buckled in, and I jogged to the entrance to make up for lost time. While I was running into the mall, I had to laugh as I couldn't help but think about what we must have looked like on the mall security video footage!

Somehow, I managed to find my friends, and I'm sure we were a *SIGHT* once we were all together! We were three groovy moms with strollers zigzagging through the mall in a line like a train, each freighting two kids. Overall the day went pretty well, despite the *DIVING* catches I had to make to save fragile items from hitting the floor, and of course, hanging up countless articles of clothing that the kids pulled off the racks as they rolled by them in the stroller. My two-year-old son wore a wet shirt most of the day because, during every diaper-changing shift for the baby, he decided to play in the sink. (Yes, I understand, most parents might panic and do everything they can to keep the kid out of the sink, but all I could think was at *LEAST* it wasn't the toilets!) Considering I don't have the new "Extension Arms for Young Moms" that I hear are just the rage, I settled for a wet shirt. We were having a *GOOD* day out.

Of course, the common phrases throughout the day included, "Get *BACK* here!" and "Don't *TOUCH* or I will put you back in the stroller," along with, "Hey! Hey! *WAIT* for mommy!", "*PLEASE* don't chew on the price tags," and "No more *WHINING*." But, really, considering the fact that we had six kids under four, all together at the mall, we seemed to be doing *PRETTY* well.

On my way out of the mall, just as I was reflecting on what a great and manageable day we were having, I passed a clearance sign, and I was like an insect headed for the bug zapper! (Moms who don't get out much have to make the most of every opportunity to find *JUST* the right deal on a shirt that hides the after-baby belly.) While in a daze, staring at the sale prices and hoping to find something in my size, I failed to notice that my two-year-old son had *unscrewed* the top to my *BRAND NEW* bottle of hair gel! When I looked down at the kids, Josh was pulling out the long pump and wiping it onto Kate's head. Kate then proceeded to spread it around with her hands. So, at nine months old my daughter was introduced to *LUXURIOUS* salon hair gel. *There will be no hope for her now!* I thought. *She'll be a girly-girl 'til the day she dies!*

    I cleaned them up with some wipes I had in the diaper bag and decided to call it a day! I think we crammed enough adventure into three-and-a-half hours for one tired mom. It was time to go home, put the kids to bed for a nap, and maybe steal a few minutes of peace and quiet to myself and recover from my "*REFRESHING*" day out.

Wonder-MOM!
By Jessica

For all those men out there who think us moms sit at home watching *Days of Our Lives*, eating bon-bons...try *THIS* day on for size. First of all, it was potty training day for Ayden. (I mean, *really*, need I say more? Anyone who has *ever* tried to train a little human being to go on the potty knows what a nightmare *THAT* can be.) However, we were actually off to a *GREAT* start. I was so proud of my little man; he wore his big boy undies all morning and kept them dry! Along with the success of dry undies, my day really *DID* start out fantastic. I got both boys dressed and fed, and even managed to make a dessert to take to a meeting I had later in the evening. And even *MORE* impressive, I managed to sweep my floors, vacuum my stairs (and I'm not even going to say how *long* it had been), clean toilets, and make my shopping list, all the while remembering to ask Ayden if he had to go potty *every two minutes. Wow!!!* I was Wonder Woman!

All was going smoothly until Zayne, my one-year-old porky kid, decided he wanted to be cranky about an hour before he was *supposed* to take his second nap. *Oh, no!* I thought, *Gotta stall him so I can lay both my boys down at the same time.* (Even Wonder Woman needs her *quiet* time!) I had done great all morning, so an hour should have been a piece of cake, *RIGHT*?!?

I threw my multitasking abilities into *FULL* throttle. I chopped some onions to make a *lovely* stir-fry for lunch, and while those were cooking I began mixing ingredients for banana bread and popped a bottle in the microwave for Zayne. (Hey, if I'm gonna *profess* to be Wonder Woman, I should probably live up to the name. *Wink*!) Oh, and did I mention I did *ALL* this with Zayne whining and hanging on my leg? His chunky diaper butt would slide and bump across the floor as I dragged him with every step.

Moments later, Ayden called me to come check his amazing creation in the sandbox. Well, of course, I *HAD* to go see his "masterpiece" 'cause he was beaming ear to ear. Upon stepping back into the kitchen my nose turned up at an *awful* burning smell. *Ahhhhhhh! The onions!!!!* I went tearing through the house to rescue them, but it was too late. Not being one to give up, I picked out the onions I thought might be salvageable. To complete my stir-fry I added peas, corn, brown rice, pink salmon, and then doused it with Tamari sauce to drown out any burnt flavor my *less than perfect* onions may have added. *Ha! Take THAT Martha Stewart!* Aside from the blackened, worm-like onions, the meal looked pretty darn *AMAZING*. But my self-pleased saunter was quickly interrupted by little toddler fingers tapping on my hip. With a disgusted look on his face

Ayden said, "Mommy, this is gross."

"Seriously, Ayden, it can't be that baaa...*YUCK!!*" My scolding was interrupted by my own taste buds. *Yup, burnt onions don't hide well.* Tossing the "responsible" mom handbook out the door we scratched lunch all together and ate popsicles.

After "lunch," it was playtime with mommy. As fun as it is to make truck noises and pretend to crash into things, I could feel naptime was right around the corner and my mind began to conjure all the *FUN* things *I* was going to do during quiet time! Oh, the possibilities!!

During a highway pileup on the Matchbox track, I noticed Ayden reaching for his buns. "Do you have to go poop? Tell me so you don't go in your underwear," I said, hoping to be preemptive. *Cleaning a tootsie roll (and not the candy kind) out of my kids undies was NOT what I had in mind for my quiet time.*

"Um...nope," he said, with a *not* so reassuring grin. Just seconds later his little eyes almost jumped out of his head and he enthusiastically said, "Yup....I *DO* have to go poop!" We ran into my bathroom, ripped his skivvy's down, and sat him on the pot. Sure enough, two little "rolls" plopped out.

"YAY!" I screamed, as I clapped my hands together. However, in the middle of our potty party I realized I didn't shut the gate to the stairway. I ran out to the hall and there was "pork-ums" just starting to peer over the edge of the tall staircase. I rescued him in one fell swoop and kicked the gate shut. *GEEZ!!!!* (I mean, sure, he has enough baby chub to break his fall, but I am glad *today* wasn't the day we were going to test just how many times he would bounce!)

I brought him back into the bathroom with me and saw that Ayden had gotten off the toilet by himself, and he was so proud. I was doing the fake "yay" face as I looked at the brown streaks on the toilet seat, hoping no dingle berries fell from his butt as he jumped around in excitement. Ayden and I went the bedroom to grab some baby wipes to get those buns squeaky clean. He began to ask when baby Zayne would poop on the potty. *BABY ZAYNE!!!!* I jumped up from wiping Ayden's bum, ran into the bathroom, and grabbed Zayne's puggy hand just before he reached for the "floating candy" he seemed to think Ayden had made *just* for him. *Eeeek!* I cringed. I flushed and quickly shut the lid, thus putting a damper on any aspirations Zayne had of eating out of the toilet bowl... today anyway. Then I walked back into the bedroom to see Ayden wiping his *OWN* butt. He was *again, so* proud. I found myself wrinkling my nose and wondering if that was dirt under his fingernails or newly acquired fecal matter. *Gross!* I looked at him and wanted to submerge his hands in a bowl of bleach. (I settled for a less chemically harmful bath instead, so in the tub they both went.) Thank goodness naptime was *MINUTES* away!!!

Whew! Like I said, bon bons & soaps? Ha, I don't *THINK* so boys! (And if you ever find us on the couch eating chocolate and watching TV with glazed eyes, it's to recover from a day like *THIS*!) I think all of us women know what *COULD* have happened if a *MAN* had been in charge. If not for Wonder Woman mom, Zayne probably would have eaten his first tootsie roll today...and not the *candy* kind.

Hmmmm, WHY do I yell so much?!?
By Jamie

My husband said to me the other day, "I think you just need to relax a little. You get so frustrated in the mornings getting the kids on the bus, and you get so upset if they don't get to bed on time. I think it would be a lot easier if you didn't yell so much."

Being the calm, understanding person I am (one who *CERTAINLY* doesn't over-personalize), I was able to look at him and calmly say, with a smile, "Ya know what, Sweetheart? You are *RIGHT*. I *am* a little overwhelmed. Maybe we could come up with some *creative* ideas together to help speed the kids up and get out the door on time in the morning." *NOPE!!!!!!* My *REAL* reaction was something like this...

"Duh! We *ALL* wish I would stop yelling! Tell me something I *don't* know! Tell me something I haven't already told myself a *MILLION* times! I mean, I was *JUST* at June Cleaver's house the other day, asking her how *SHE* does it. Ya know what *I* think would help? How about if when I say calmly the *FIRST* time, 'Okay, kids, hurry up, it's time to go,' they *ACTUALLY* pick up their pace and get on task? No, instead we have to fill up the water bottles, which, mind you, were part of the after school routine to be done *YESTERDAY*! Of course, *YESTERDAY*, when I asked, 'Did you guys finish your routines?' everyone's answer was, 'Yes.' Hmmm. My mistake. I am *SURE* they did all their jobs, and then *MYSTERIOUSLY* the water bottles emptied themselves and jumped back in the drawers. That is the kids' argument anyway." *Ya, I'm the irrational one!!!*

"And then Timmy can't find his shoes, Josh can't find his coat, 'cause heaven forbid we put them away when we take them off! And if it's not that, it's me playing referee in the bathroom 'cause Kate isn't happy that Josh's hairbrush is in her way, or maybe his elbow touched hers while they were brushing their teeth. By now I have said *FOUR* times, that it is time to go, and *YES*, it isn't so sweet anymore! Finally, I shove them out the door, dig out my sweet voice again to say, 'I love you guys. Have a good day,' and then shut the door with a deep sigh thinking, *I will be sweeter this afternoon.*

The *NEXT* few hours of my day consist of cleaning the kitchen, laundry, sweeping, changing Bo, getting Bo *OUT* of my folded laundry, re-folding it, stopping Bo from drawing on the walls, putting Bo in time-out, feeding Bo lunch, cleaning Bo, and cleaning the kitchen AGAIN! Back to the laundry, cleaning my bathroom, getting Bo out from under my bathroom sink, putting everything *BACK* under the sink, stopping Bo from flushing things down the toilet, putting Bo in timeout *AGAIN*! Changing Bo (but Bo doesn't *WANT* to be changed), putting him in timeout 'til he's ready, *FINALLY* changing him.

Then I have to go pick up the kids from school. As I walk to the van,

I see the cat vomit in the cat bed that I *TOLD* you about a *WEEK* ago! Of course, my multitasking mind digs out the argument I had with you about why I *didn't WANT* a pet, my case being I didn't need anything else to *feed* or *CLEAN UP AFTER!*" (*Pause rant.* Michael's argument had been that it would teach the kids responsibility, and *they* would take care of the cat, so just *relax. Resume* completely *justified* rant.) "I get to the school, forget to put Bo in the stroller, grab a box of work from Kate's teacher ('cause I am an awesome, helping room mom). Now with my hands full, I *chase* Bo through the hallways. Finally, I pile the box on Kate and just carry the wiggling child out the door!

Get home, walk by the cat vomit *again*, roll my eyes, put back packs away, feed kids a snack, and then start on chores. *Argue* with the kids about *WHY* we have to do chores, *argue* about *WHY* they have so much work to do, then I, of course, give my speech about how when I was a kid I had to vacuum the whole house 'uphill both ways', *RIGHT?!* After they do their chores, we *argue* about WHY they aren't done sufficiently. Do them *AGAIN*! *Finally* it's TV time and kids disappear. I take this time to prepare dinner, which, yes, *IS* easier now that Bo actually *WATCHES* a movie with the kids rather than cry at my ankles. So this works well, and I begin to feel like I'm getting back on top of things again.

Eat dinner. Clean up after dinner. *Argue* with kids about *WHY* they have to help clean up the kitchen. When their jobs are done, I send them off to do the bedtime routine, and I finish the kitchen *myself*. Head upstairs, *argue* with Kate about *WHY* she is reading before she has brushed her teeth and picked up her clothes, *argue* with Bo about *WHY* it's time for bed. Put Timmy and Bo to bed, *finally* put Kate to bed. You and Josh play video games 'til Josh's bedtime and at 9:00pm I remind you it's time for Josh to go to bed. Ten minutes later I have to remind you guys *AGAIN*. I go finish up laundry. Five minutes later I yell down the stairs that it is *now* fifteen minutes *AFTER* Josh's bedtime.

Finally, Josh is in bed (insert exhausted sigh) and I look around to see what I must finish before I can crawl into bed and *maybe* watch a little TV. Then off to sleep I go. Up at 1:00 am 'cause Timmy's got to pee. Up at 3:00 am 'cause Kate had a bad dream. Then the alarm rings at 6:55am, and we start *ALL OVER AGAIN...*

"Ya, I *SO* need to find a way to stop yelling so much!"

Are we there yet?

By Jamie

My sister and I seem to find ourselves on many, what you might call, "adventurous excursions." It doesn't matter *WHERE* we are going—it could be a five day vacation together or a simple trip to the McDonald's play land--it's just bound to be an *ADVENTURE* or a *SCENE*, whichever way you choose to see it, and sometimes we don't see the "funny" until *LONG* after the "adventure" is over. This time our families were taking a three-and-a-half hour trip to Boyne Falls, Michigan, for the weekend. We were *REALLY* looking forward to three days away from household duties. Just us lounging by the pool, with one eye open, of course, to be sure we came home with the same number of kids we left with. (That seems to be our motto these days!)

This time our "foolproof" plan was to leave a day before the boys and enjoy some *GIRL* gab. It was simple: leave in the morning, rent Grey's Anatomy Season 3 at our local video store (we were in the middle of a Grey's-athon), drive to Boyne, unload, and have the kids all tucked in bed by 8:00 pm. We would then curl up on the couch to veg out in front of our favorite drama series. No problem, right?

WRONG. The first sign of trouble showed up the night before when I realized my tags on my van were *expired.* I thought Michael renewed them for me like he does every year, but for some reason he thought *I* renewed them *myself* this year. (Huh, AS IF!?!) So, the morning of our trip, the kids and I loaded up and went to the Secretary of State, which was 15 minutes in the absolute *OPPOSITE* direction of our ultimate destination. *No problem! We are going on vacation. NOTHING is gonna get me down!* Just a minor detour and we were on the road...legally.

Picking Jess and Ayden up, we realized Jake went to work with Ayden's car seat in his truck. *No problem, it was on our way, and we are going on VACATION!* We were able to drive...legally...because my van had the 5-point harness child seats built into the bench seat, but Jess figured Ayden would sleep better in his own car seat. She was probably right. However, I *DID* roll my eyes and wonder if he would *ACTUALLY* fall asleep with my *FOUR* kids in the van. Especially since the kid sitting next to him was...Bo! He was my loudest child, yet again, no worries, *right?* We were going on vacation!!! Just a stop to the video store and it would be smooth sailing from there.

"What?! Wait a minute! Did you say you don't *HAVE* Greys Anatomy season 3?!?" My jaw dropped open and my shoulders slumped. The employee blinked real slow and chomped a couple times on the pink gum she had in her mouth.

"Nope...don't have it," she said, even slower than she blinked.

"Seriously, who *ELSE* is watching old seasons of Grey's Anatomy?" I said, as I wrinkled my eyebrows and threw up my hands. A bit like a drug addict being denied her next fix, I started to hyperventilate slightly as my brain worked overtime to figure out *HOW* we were gonna get our show. The poor gum-chewing clerk had no idea that this was just the beginning of my disappointed rant. "And season 3, at that? I mean seriously?!? Why not season 1 or season 4? Somebody else just *HAPPENED* to rent season 3?" By this time I was shaking my head and both hands were on the counter. "Not to mention they had to rent it *THIS WEEKEND!*" My hands hit the counter as I vented the last two syllables, "FOR *REAL*?!?" I then laughed, only to keep the clerk from calling the men in white coats to come pick me up. I could see the unconvinced look on her face, so I walked toward the door, shaking my head and smiling a fake smile. I couldn't help, but rant on as I reached the exit. "Only my sister and me," I exclaimed, waving my pointer finger in the air. "Yup, this would *ONLY* happen to *US*," I said over my shoulder to the clerk, who probably at this point had her finger *HOVERING* over the panic button. Once again, I convinced myself that we were on *VACATION* and NOTHING WAS GONNA GET ME DOWN! C'est la vie...right? We hit the road figuring we could search the GPS on the way for another video store, perhaps closer to our destination, and attempt *NOT* to make a scene.

Finally we were on the road! *Yay! Let the sister gabbing begin.* Well, *KINDA.* Much of our energy was spent trying to keep Bo from being so noisy and keep the older kids in the back from laughing out loud at their movie, thus waking Ayden up. Despite our attempts to quietly get their attention, they remained entranced by their show. Ayden was somehow managing to sleep through all the laughing, but finally, to get the kids' attention, Jessie snapped her fingers and Ayden jolted awake. Ironically, the kids in the back *STILL* never heard us.

Other than Ayden not getting a very long nap, things were still going pretty smoothly and we started searching the GPS for video stores. "Mom, I have to poop really bad," Timmy said, as he squinched up his eyebrows almost as if he was in pain. And about that time Ayden started crying. Jess and I looked at each other and knew we *HAD* to pull over.

"Next exit there is a McDonald's...get over in the right lane," Jess told me. I carefully weaved in-between cars. "Oh no, get back over...the exit is on the left..who would put it on the..."

"Jessie, am I clear?? *JESS*??" I was trying to cross over *THREE* lanes knowing there is a *HUGE* blind spot on the driver side of my van.

"Um...no wait...you got a car..wait...ok, you're clear...YOU'RE CLEAR...why aren't you moving?".

"We missed it," I said.

"That's alright, we will just hit the next one," she said, with a shrug of her shoulders. At this point, Timmy was almost in *TEARS* because he couldn't hold it any longer and Ayden was *SCREAMING*. Bo was starting to complain about being bored and Kate started saying she was hungry. Jess grabbed the Garmin and found the next Mcdonald's was 20 miles up the highway. *OMG!* We had a good 20-minute drive ahead of us! (Up north in Michigan, civilization *really* decreases; you do *NOT* want to miss your exit!)

We were just quiet. At this point there was nothing to be done, but brace ourselves for *INSANITY* to kick in. Though we were frazzled as can be, we somehow made it to the next exit and swerved into a McDonald's *JUST* in time for Timmy and I to jump out of the van, to the restroom hoping to make it, as Jess let Ayden out of his car seat for a bit. We decided to grab the kids some dinner and jump back onto the highway.

Now that there were no crying kids, Jess started searching the Garmin again for video stores. After about 15 minutes, we thought we should check our "whereabouts". Strangely enough, the GPS was telling us to turn around...over and over and over. We figured it *MUST* be confused. However, when we retyped the address of our hotel again, we discovered that our little emergency restroom stop was *ACTUALLY the EXIT* we were *SUPPOSED* to take to our *HOTEL*. BAH!!!!! *SERIOUSLY????*

We turned around as soon as we could, and by this time we are both tired and ready to be on the couch with a movie. Had we been paying attention, we would have already arrived! The McDonald's we stopped at was only *TEN minutes* away from our destination. However, we were now 25 minutes away. By this time, Ayden and Bo were getting *BORED* and *CRANKY* (and, let me tell ya, their *MOMS* weren't doing much better!). We were giving them *ANYTHING* we thought would entertain them.

Finally, after exhausting every other option in the van, we tossed Ayden a lid from the McDonald's cup. (Now, yes, this is *NOT* something I would recommend, but we were just grasping for anything that would stop the crying.) It actually worked great for awhile... until he started *CHOKING*. (And *THAT* would be why I don't recommend it. *Wink!*) Come to find out, he had bitten off a chunk of the plastic and was gagging. Jess was up and out of her seat in a flash, and I pulled off to the side of the road. (It was a good thing we were no longer on the highway!) Moments before I put the van in park, Ayden threw up his *WHOLE* dinner, along with the plastic chunk. *At least we got the chunk out! Yay!* But as for the car seat, did I *FORGET* to mention that Jess had given him a *SPINACH* smoothie *BEFORE* we left home? As if barf isn't gross *ENOUGH*, now it was green and looked like a decomposing compost pile!

FINALLY, exhausted and with the smell of barf *OOZING* out of the van, we arrived at our vacation spot. At the check-in desk, we found out about our next "adventure". We were on the second floor of our Swiss-looking units that, of course, did *NOT* have an elevator. So, now these two moms and five kids had to haul our luggage up two flights of stairs. *SERIOUSLY?!? We just HAD to leave the boys and come a day earlier rather than staying a day late???* The suitcases would have at least rolled down the stairs a lot easier than they rolled up!

Jess put Ayden and Bo in the tub while I dragged up the suitcases. *Wonder Woman!* By the time I pulled the last bit of luggage to the room, Jess was drying off Ayden. (Yes, *THAT'S* how *LONG* it took "Wonder Wom-

I NEED CHOCOLATE...STAT

an" to carry up the luggage of two moms and their five kids! Afterwards, I wasn't feeling so bad about my plans to indulge in snacks and lie by the pool all weekend because I already *GOT* my workout!) I huffed and puffed my luggage up to my room and grabbed my wet streaker as he tried to run by. As I laid him down to get dressed, I noticed it looked like he stepped in dog poo. What the *HECK*? I lifted up his legs to get a better look between his cheeks. "YOU'VE GOT TO BE KIDDING ME!" I said, louder than expected. Still holding Bo's legs in the air, I looked over my shoulder and traced the brown footprints all the way back to the bathroom.

I'm on vacation...I'm on vacation...I am ON VACATION. I was *DETERMINED* to keep my happy-go-lucky attitude. I kept thinking that, any minute, production people would *BUST* through the door and announce that we were on the show "You've Been Punked". After cleanup, it was already 8pm, and we were *NOWHERE* near curled up on the couch watching TV. I think we both wanted to *CRY*.

Somehow, we managed to get all five kids into bed, and we decided Jess would hold down the fort while I went to pick up just the essentials at the grocery store. And by "essentials" I mean some *HARD CORE CHOCOLATE*. It seemed we might just finally be on the home stretch of the day's "adventures"! The store was only *SEVEN* minutes away, so it wouldn't take too long. Problem was I, being directionally *CHALLENGED*, took a couple wrong turns and it took me 20 minutes to get to the store. However, my spirits were lifted when I noticed a video rental store *RIGHT* next to the grocery store, and they *HAD* Grey's Anatomy season 3!

Things were looking up...*FINALLY*. I headed back to the room with some munchies and couldn't wait to plop myself on the couch, and I even *SOMEHOW* managed to make it

Buy more sticky notes!

home without getting lost! To hurry things along, I *enabled* my "one trip wonder" abilities and carried *ALL* the bags in at once. During this attempt, I dropped one bag, which contained the *ONLY* glass container I bought. I couldn't drop the bag with the cereal or bread!?! *Nope*, I was lucky enough to *SHATTER* a jar of applesauce in the parking lot, just when I was *SO* close to relaxing!

Once I was finished cleaning up the parking lot mess, I walked through the door to our room, still carrying the aroma of puke from my van, with applesauce in my hair, and shot my sister a look. "You are *NEVER* going to believe this," I started to say.

Jess stopped me by saying, "Oh, no...I think I *WILL*."

"But we're on vacation, right?" I said.

"Haha! You call **this** *VACATION*??" she replied, as she took some bags out of my hands. We shared a good, needed *LAUGH* and finally plopped down on the couch. It was 11pm, but, after all we'd been through, we were *DETERMINED* to watch an episode of Grey's Anatomy, with a bag of kettle cooked potato chips and a *PILE* of chip dip! Then we finished the night off with (yes, *YOU* guessed it) *CHOCOLATE*!

Bad Days and Silver Linings
By Jamie

Talk about your "gotta have some *HARD CORE* chocolate" days, *THIS* was *ONE* of them! It had just been one of *THOSE* days from the start. I woke up with a cold accompanied by a headache. Fortunately, Michael took the older three kids to school, and I was able to convince Bo to watch cartoons for awhile so I could take some Tylenol and lay down a *BIT* longer. The rest of the afternoon mostly consisted of laundry and cleaning, a typical Monday for me. Not really any big deal. Just going through the motions, hoping this head cold would clear soon. Finally, it was time to pick up my older kids from school. I had made it to the afternoon (*yay!*), and now the kids would be home to entertain Bo (*double yay!*), so it was all smooth sailing from here, for sure. I had even decided on frozen pizza for dinner. Yup, things were looking *UP*!

As Bo and I headed to the van, I saw our cat in the front window *SITTING ON MY DASHBOARD*! In that moment, Michael's words from that morning came back to me. "Have you seen the cat? I couldn't find him last night or this morning. Is he in the house somewhere?" Well, I found him, and the day just took a *MAJOR* turn for the worse! I was *SCARED* to open the van door. It was safe to assume he had been in there *ALL* night, and I was not sure how *BIG* that cat's bladder was, but I was pretty sure it wasn't big *ENOUGH*. Sure enough, as I opened the door, the incredibly awful odor of stale cat pee *BILLOWED* out and *HIT* me in the *FACE*! Oh...my...*GOSH*! The pet that I *DIDN'T* really want, 'cause I *DIDN'T* want something *ELSE* to clean up after, took a *WIZ...* in... my...*VAAAAAAAAAAAAN!!!* (*NOT* my happiest moment.)

Being the calm, cool, and collected person that I *ALWAYS* am (*wink*!), I called my husband at work and left a *VERY CHEERFUL* message using *ALL* my *POLITE* words (as you can imagine), never *ONCE* reminding him that I *NEVER* wanted this *STUPID* cat to begin with! (Yeah, okay, it didn't exactly go like that, but what I really said isn't printable. Lol!) He called me back and informed me that when he locked up the previous night he found the van door open and shut it for me. (Aw, how kind of him, right?) He didn't know the *CAT* was in there, and he *ASSURED* me that he and the kids would clean up the mess when he came home.

When I picked up the kids and answered their questions about the interesting odor in the van, I informed them that "Project Cat Pee" would be *THEIR* responsibility when Dad got home. Their whining instantly filled the van. "Why do *WE* have to clean up after the cat? He is your cat, too. *You* should have to help."

Yeah. I *PROBABLY* should have waited until the steam quit blowing out my ears to respond. *NOPE!* Instead, I declared in my *NOT VERY NICE* mom voice, "I *NEVER* wanted the cat because I KNEW when it came to cleaning up pet messes, I was sure *YOU* kids would complain! So, if you *REALLY* don't want to clean it up, let me know and I will *GIVE* the cat away *TOMORROW*!!!!"

After my explosion and threat to put the cat up for adoption, they got quiet, and when Michael returned home that evening they all went to work while I looked for my hidden stash of chocolate. Fortunately (*trying* to find a silver lining in all of this), most of the pee was on one of the van rugs. Once *THAT* was removed the smell was faint, and faint was *WAY* better than the very offensive smell it *HAD* been. I suppose it wasn't the end of the world, even though it seemed so at the time, though it was almost the *END* of the *CAT!* I was so thankful the cat hadn't sprayed one of my seats! (Yet another silver lining.) If he *HAD*, foster care was *FOR SURE* in his future! (Lol!)

A challenge for you: "Value Before Chocolate"

Adversity! I gotta say, after the most challenging days this momma LOVES her chocolate. (Well, I actually love chocolate any day and every day.) However, as much as I hate to admit it, we actually do need adversity in our lives. Whether it's crazy situations like missing a flight, our kids clogging the toilet with toy cars, or considerably more serious challenges, such as landing in the emergency room with our child or teaching them how to handle a bullying issue at school. Whatever the case may be, it's our adversities that drive us to learn and progress as human beings.

Sometimes our adversity helps us develop patience. Other times, our adversity compels us to be vulnerable with those we love, creating an even stronger bond with one another. There can also be times where we simply learn what *NOT* to do *NEXT* time. Lol! No matter what, the secret to surviving our adversities is to find *VALUE* in them. In order to find value, we ultimately choose to *learn* from our adversity and embrace it as part of our progression. Rather than causing us to feel defeated, our adversity actually becomes a tool when we allow the experience to develop us as a person.

Value Before Chocolate Challenge:
Throughout this next week, as you come face to face with personal challenges, decide how you can create Value within them.

Examples:

Adversity: I missed my exit on the highway.
Value: I will learn to be patient and, maybe if I'm lucky, I'll see some new terrain or a great garage sale along the drive. (Lol!)

Adversity: A more serious and personal example, of my own, is the adversity I faced when my parents divorced. I just couldn't imagine what *good* would come out of such a heartbreaking experience.
Value: I finally decided that if nothing else, one day I would be a shoulder to lean on and provide support for someone else going through a similar adversity.

Adversity: _____

Value: _____

Adversity: _____

Value: _____

Adversity: _____

Value: _____

PART 5

God said he wouldn't put me through anything I couldn't handle
Does He have me confused with someone else?

What are you hanging on to?
By Jamie

We all tend to hang on to *stuff* that we need to let go of. Me? I am hanging on to a little two-piece, camouflage, matching shorts and tank top outfit, worn by my son Timmy when he was three years old. I can't help but think back to when I put him in this outfit *that* morning. At the time, I didn't realize the irony of putting him in a pattern that's purpose was to hide in plain sight!

It was a sunny day in June. The kids were out of school and we needed groceries. I remember preparing my kids for this grocery run—the day is etched in my brain *FOREVER*. My fourth baby, Bo, was just two months old, and when he was first born, my mom would watch the kids when I went to the grocery store. But, I wanted to be able to shop successfully on my own without the help of a babysitter, so I decided I was ready to take on the job myself. Before entering the doors of the grocery store, I gave *each* kid a task. My oldest was to read the list while the other two would put the items in the cart and the baby would, hopefully, sleep the whole time (wouldn't *THAT* be a dream?!?). I explained to them how we needed to work as a team and they agreed to the "mission".

They did *AWESOME*! They all did their jobs and helped me tremendously. We were able to finish the whole list in record time. I gave a sigh of relief and felt such power from our accomplishment. While the kids were waiting for the groceries to be bagged and put in the cart, they stepped across the aisle to play with the buttons on a vending machine. My three-year-old was hanging with his brother (seven years old) and sister (six years old), pushing buttons like a pro. Even though they were only a few yards away, I kept watching them while loading my cart, just to be sure they were all there.

Finally, just when I paid the cashier and was ready to go, Josh and Kate came to the sides of the cart, and I asked, "Where is Timmy?" They both looked around. *WHAT?!? THEY don't know where he is? He was JUST with them!!!* I began scanning a bigger area, wondering if he had wandered to another checkout lane, but *no* Timmy. At this point I was a little nervous, but not freaking out. I thought, in reality, he was probably right there *somewhere*. As time kept ticking, *PANIC* began setting in. I remember telling the workers that I was beginning to freak out and I needed to find my son before I started to lose my mind.

"I need to find my son! Please, *LOCK* your doors! I *NEED* to find my son," I kept saying.

"Okay, ma'am. What is he wearing?" a worker responded.

"Um, I don't know," I stammered, "Oh, dang it! I don't remem... Wait! He is wearing camouflage. I need to find him, *PLEASE*. Please *SHUT* and *LOCK* your doors! I need my son," I said pleadingly, with tears rolling steadily down my cheeks.

I remember pleading with God, *Please God, please bring him to me. This is one of those experiences I CAN'T handle. PLEASE, don't let this happen.*

"Ok ma'am. How old is he?" the worker asked.

As I said the words out loud it only made me even more aware of how fragile he was. "He is three," I said. And then I screamed, "He is ONLY THR-E-E!!! I NEED to find my son! Please, shut your doors! LOCK YOUR DAMN DOORS!" I shouted.

As time kept passing, I began to feel like one of those people in the movies when everything happens around them but it's all muffled 'cause they're in shock. People's voices around me sounded like far-off echoes. I remember hearing the words, "We have a code..." but didn't hear what kind of code it was. I just remember thinking, *Oh, God, we have a code. This is REALLY happening. It is not a dream, and we have a code.*

I could see people staring at me, but I didn't care. I could see my other two kids standing by the cart looking at me with innocence and confusion. I remember thinking of the trauma I must be causing them, but couldn't stop. I had *NO* ability to be *CALM*. I just knew I wouldn't leave them standing there alone. I just kept yelling over and over, "Shut the damn doors!!" I kept screaming, begging and pleading, with tears pouring down my face, "Please, I *NEED* my son, please *SHUT* your *DOORS!*"

"Ma'am, we are doing everything we can," the lady told me.

"No, you're *NOT!* You could *LOCK* your *DOORS* so someone can't take him *OUT* of here!" I snapped at her.

As time kept slipping away I found myself trying to reconcile with the fact that he *might* be gone. I wondered how I would survive the torture of not knowing where he was and what he was going through. And as my mind started to fade to a very dark, quiet place of hopelessness, off in the distance I heard someone say, "We found him. Here he is. He is right here." My knees *BUCKLED* and I hit the floor.

They walked him up to me, and I just looked into his sweet eyes as he peered at me with a questioning, yet concerned expression. He was quiet. I think he could sense the gravity of the moment, but he was unaware of the severity of the situation and how the fear of what *could* have happened had seriously shaken my world. As if he knew exactly what I needed, he walked up to me and put his arms around my neck and hugged me. When I think back on that day, I can still feel his little arms around my neck. I can feel his hair on my cheek. I just cried for a moment with him in my arms, and my two older kids joined our embrace.

After I collected myself, we made our way to the parking lot, where I climbed into my van and *SOBBED*. That night, when I tucked Timmy into bed, I kissed his cheek, thanking God that I *STILL* could.

I *NEVER* put him in that outfit again. In fact, he received a different pair of camouflage shorts as a gift, and it took me till the end of the summer to let him wear them. I think he only wore them once before it was too cold to wear shorts anymore. I later shared with my life coach, Dean Nixon, that I still had the outfit. Until then, I hadn't told anyone. He said something to me I didn't expect. "You know that hanging on to the outfit won't keep it from ever happening again?"

Until that moment, I didn't even realize *WHY* I was keeping that outfit, but I knew he was right. I know it sounds silly to think, but there is a *PART* of me that feels like hanging onto those clothes will give me *CONTROL*. *Somehow* they will keep me more vigilant. They will keep me from making a mistake and losing him or any of my children *EVER* again. As if hanging on to my biggest fear or biggest mistake will keep it from happening. When Dean said those words to me, I could feel the fake sense of control slip through my fingertips. A wave of fear, sadness, and pain flooded over me. I could see the *TRUTH* of his statement. *No, it won't, but to be honest I am not ready to let it go.* I told Dean I wasn't sure when, or if, I would throw them out. He answered, "You will when you are ready." And, for now, I just have to leave it at that.

So what are *YOU* hanging on to? Is it a set of clothes, a book, a letter, or some sort of trinket that reminds you of a dark time in your life that you feel guilty about or are afraid of? Something you keep to remind yourself to *NEVER* let it happen again?

Sometimes it is good to hang on to things that remind you of events in your life. The question is, are you hanging on in *LOVE*...or *FEAR*?

To this day, I have to make a conscious choice to put my kids in the hands of my Maker. It is only my faith that keeps the panic from running my life. I tell ya, this parenthood stuff is the most *AMAZING*, rewarding job, but it is also the hardest, *SCARIEST* job I will *EVER* have.

One of those days you want to forget.
By Jessica

When Ayden was two years old, we were introduced to MRSA ("mersa"). For those of you who haven't had the *PLEASURE* of such an introduction, MRSA is a *serious* staph infection that the lucky host will basically carry to the grave. It reveals itself through extremely painful boils and then, finally, when you think the *LAST* one has gone, a month later you find yourself daunting the door way of the doctor's office once again. I have become *SO* experienced with it the pharmacy at our local store knows me by name! In fact, sometimes they will see me walk through the door and say, "Aww... they have MRSA *again?*"

I had become quite the professional at identifying the boils at their earliest state and found if I covered them with antibacterial ointment and a band-aid right away, after a couple days they would disappear. *FINALLY*, we were antibiotic free for two months and I was beginning to get a glimpse of the light at the end of the tunnel. And *THEN* I was thrown a curve ball. Apparently, the MRSA had gone "incognito". I looked at Ayden's knee one day and wondered where he had gotten what looked like a big bruise. I pushed on it (like any *good* mother would do! Lol!), and he started crying. Considering the fact he was two years old, I knew I probably wouldn't figure out *WHICH* tumble was the cause, so I just rolled my eyes, assuming it would fade. When he started limping a couple days later, I decided to take him with me to Zayne's one-week well visit.

Oh, yeah, did I mention I had a *BRAND NEW BABY* while we were battling this plague?

Ugh.

So, there I was with a two-year-old and a one-week-old in the doctor's office. That's always tons of *NOT* fun. Thank *GOODNESS* my mom accompanied me that day!

When the doctor was finished with Zayne, I asked her about getting an x-ray of Ayden's knee, thinking he might have a sprain or something. She took *ONE* look at it and left the room without an explanation. My mom and I shared confused glances, and moments later the doctor returned with a nurse. They were wearing surgery gowns and placed a handful of instruments down on the examining bed! *What?!?* I could feel the *PANIC* start to permeate my *ENTIRE* being. My "mama bear" instincts began to stand at attention as I felt the urge to grab my little man and just *RUN*. I am *SURE* it didn't help that I was sleep-deprived and hormonal from just having a baby. I told myself, *If the doctor is THIS serious about getting this done, I should probably start mustering up some sort of courage for my two-year-old,* who had no idea the amount of pain he was about to experience.

So, I tried my best to distract Ayden with conversation. However, when they laid him down and began positioning his legs while I held his head, he *KNEW* something was wrong. I began to see the fear build in his eyes. At that moment, I honestly didn't know *WHAT* they were going to do; I just knew it *WASN'T* going to be fun or even be something I would *EVER* want to remember. He began to cry as they put a needle in his knee to numb the area. I tried to talk about McDonald's and the play-land we could go to as soon as we were done. Tears were now *STREAMING* down each side of his face and his lips were purple from the lack of air he was taking in. I held his cheek to mine and simply *CRIED* with him.

With my cheek never leaving his, I peered at the doctor just in time to see her push a blade into my child's knee. Ayden *SCREAMED* at this point, and I could hardly *BREATHE*. I held him tight and whispered through my own tears, "Mommy loves you baby. You are *SO* strong. We are *ALMOST* done." I looked down to the doctor again and said sternly through gritted teeth, "How much longer?" No response. Again I went back to consoling my little boy.

After a couple more minutes of holding his head to mine, he looked at me, took a deep breath in, and screamed, "Mommy!"

I turned to the doctor and yelled, "Enough!....Enough!...We are *DONE!*"

The doctor replied, "We are..we are....sorry sweetie." They put bandages on it and I picked him up and held him *SO* tight. I felt *horrible*. I felt *helpless*. I felt like the *WORST* mother. I kept telling Ayden how sorry I was and that it was over. I literally *STORMED* out of the office trying to hold it somewhat together. My mom carried the baby. No *WAY* was I letting my oldest out of my arms. Not after *THIS*.

I collected myself enough to call my husband to tell him we were right around the corner from McDonald's, where he planned on meeting us. Over the phone, I told him of our horrifying experience, and when he pulled in the McDonald's drive at the same time as us, he grabbed Ayden and pulled him close. Ayden's knee was so sore we ended up leaving McDonald's because he couldn't walk on it. On our way home, he fell asleep, and I began to cry. The *ENTIRE* scene began to replay through my mind.

Everything.

I searched for ways I could have made that situation better. *Why didn't I make them wait until his knee was completely numb? They are doctors! They should have known. Because if it were numb, then SURELY he wouldn't have screamed the way he did when the blade cut into his skin, right?* My mom-guilt was at *FULL* throttle. I sat there emotionally drained, trying to decide if I was still the person who should be his mom. *I can't protect him from this MRSA. What if he gets it again? What if we have to lance some other appendage? I can't do it. I won't.*

That night, after he went to bed, I just stood over his crib and quietly cried, saying the words, "I'm sorry."

Did he know how *SORRY* I was?

Did he know it *HAD* to be done?

Did he know if I could have gone through it for him I *WOULD* have?

I went to bed that night telling God to give it to me, asking Him to clear Ayden's little body of this horrible virus and please just **give...it... to...me**. I lay there reprimanding God, asking Him *HOW* He could let this happen. It wasn't fair. He was too young.

Finally, I began trying to let myself start the process of falling asleep. It didn't work. Every time I closed my eyes, all I could see was Ayden's little face in pain. And I was *helpless*. Morning couldn't come soon enough. I just wanted to watch him be a normal kid again. I wanted to hold him and let him know that I would protect him. That I would stand up for him. That he is safe in my arms...and always *WILL* be...even if I can do nothing else, but hold his hand. As a mom, I hate that I can't protect my kids from everything, but I can walk through it with them, and no matter the trial they will *know* I love them.

To trust, not to trust?

By Jessica

I was at the pediatrician's office *AGAIN*. Being the proud mom of two young children, I felt as though I *lived* there. This time I was there for Zayne, my six-month-old, because I was pretty sure he was starting to get an ear infection. My pediatrician was out for the month overseas, so I was stuck with a doctor we didn't know filling in for her. After she finished looking in his ears, I asked her to look at his eyes. (Ever since Zayne was two months old his eyes would quiver back and forth rapidly a couple times a day, and now it had become pretty regular.) She pulled her light out and began examining his eyes. I was assuming she would just tell me to go to the ophthalmologist, but was hoping she would know what it was and could save me a trip. She turned to me and began giving me a brief history on what it was called and how normal it was, and then she ended with, "But I am going to set up an MRI to simply make sure there isn't a tumor on the optic nerve."

Hmmm? A what?!? Did she just say TUMOR?!? Mind you, he was only six months old and was still nursing, so naturally my hormones were not *ANYWHERE* near normal levels, but I think *anyone* would react strongly to those scary words. I blinked a couple times and tried to replay her words. "I'm sorry...did you say MRI?" I asked, blinking away tears.

"Yes, just to be sure." She began talking to me again, but I could only see her lips moving. The tears began to well, and I felt the room start to shrink. I couldn't *BREATHE*. I wanted to hold my baby and simply *CRY*. I walked out of the examining room in a daze. After going through the motions of paying yet another co-pay, I bundled Zayne up and took him out to the car, all the while trying to comprehend what just happened. I reflected back to the day he was born...

"How much does he weigh?" I heard my husband ask the nurse, who just took my twenty-second-old son over to the scale. "Nine pounds three ounces! He's a big boy!" she exclaimed. *No wonder I was so huge!* They plopped him into my arms, all wrapped up like a little pig in a blanket. He actually kind of looked like a little pig, all fat and purple. *I did it.* After going through labor with my first son, I didn't think I *EVER* wanted to do it again, but I did it!! I had another one of these little people whom I would *SO* willingly give my life for. He was *perfect!* That *moment was perfect!*

And now I was sitting here trying to wrap my head around an MRI. You can imagine what was going through my mind...*PANIC* basically. Sheer panic. *Not even SIX months old, and the word TUMOR has already popped its ugly self into his life.* My thoughts kept fluctuating from, *"It's nothing!"* to, *"My child may have an inoperable tumor!"* I told myself right then and there that Grey's Anatomy would *NO* longer be at the top of my list of shows to watch. However, I found myself actually wishing Derek Shephard *was* a real brain surgeon.

We got home and I put my oldest to bed and then simply sat on the floor staring at my baby. Little Zayne. I found myself *WISHING* I could go back to that first day of his life. Back to when everything was *GOOD*. Back to when he was just a fat baby and all I had to do was feed him, hold him, and love him. I had just popped him out and life was good. He was my *WORLD* at that moment. Ten pudgy fingers and ten pudgy toes. He was a bit *slimy*, but still perfect.

I don't really know how I got through the next couple of weeks, but I did. Life seems to work that way; it just goes *ON*. I had to reel my mind in more than once when it would flood with possible scenarios. I pictured my child having brain surgery and then the recovery. Or, even worse, having an inoperable tumor and having to watch him endure chemo. Or it might be a cancerous tumor that they couldn't cure and he only had six months to live. My mind went to *EVERY* horrible ending possible. And even though the days were hard to get through, at times, I still got through them.

We scheduled the MRI for a Friday so my husband could take the day off and come with me. The night before that appointment, I tried to surrender myself to what was going to happen. They would have to give him an I.V., and I imagined listening to him cry if they couldn't find a vein. *How many times will they have to stick him with the needle?* They would put him to sleep as he lay in my arms. I kept imaging what it would feel like to have my bubbly little baby simply go to sleep in my embrace. To watch him as he sucked on his bink and simply closed his eyes. To feel his breath deepen. To feel the fear rise up with in me. *Is he going to wake up?* What if he stops breathing? To look at my sleeping angel and then have to hand him over to a *STRANGER*. To watch them take him away from me, not knowing what they would find. It *SICKENED* me.

Thursday night, at 2:34 a.m., he woke up with a fever of 101 degrees. I was up with him all throughout the night and immediately called the nurse in the morning. They told me they don't put little ones under anesthesia when they are sick because it's too much of a risk. So, no MRI *that* day. We rescheduled for the following Friday. The next week came and he was still fighting a cold. I decided, in the meantime, to go ahead and take him to see the neurologist. He said Zayne was developing normally and didn't show any signs of concern. We were also able to see the ophthalmologist before the MRI. This was the doctor I couldn't *wait* to get into. If *ANYONE* knew something, it would be *HIM*.

That was a visit I will *NEVER* forget. I was sitting in the chair, holding Zayne, while the doctor made all sorts of animal sounds to get him to focus. The doctor was *AMAZING*! Zayne *DID* amazing!! I held my breath as he finished the exam and started giving us his diagnosis. "There is nothing out of the ordinary here. You have seen the worst of it and he might even grow out of it. From what I can see, there is no reason he can't have 20/20 vision when he gets older. I don't see any reason for an MRI."

No reason for an MRI? Really? The *RELIEF* was *OVERWHELMING*. I didn't realize how much tension I was holding onto until my tears of relief began to form in my eyes. I smiled at my husband, who was also overcome with emotion taking in the news. We both took a breath for the first time in weeks. My body began to relax, and I felt an overwhelming sense of peace. I wanted to lean over and kiss that doctor. I felt my head rise a little higher. Life was going to go on…normally. I didn't have to worry. I could go back to being a mom of two beautiful boys, which was as rewarding as the day I gave birth to them! The ride home was tranquil.

Have faith!

Even after all the good news, I still had thoughts of going to see someone else or insist on an MRI, but I had a small thought reminding me that we had already scheduled the MRI two times before this visit. I had to believe these events were taking place for a reason. As I peeked back on my little boy, asleep in his car seat, I knew he had no idea of everything that was going on. Life was *GREAT* in his mind. He had a full belly, bink in his mouth, and was all cozy in his blanket. And in that moment, I felt God's peace. As parents, it's hard to let go of the fact that we *AREN'T* always in control, and *THAT'S* where I have to choose to believe that God loves my children more than I even know how. Even *IF* things changed, and an MRI was needed down the road, for *that* day I allowed all of my worrying and stressing from the past couple weeks to simply be put to rest, and I knew that *WHATEVER* the road ahead… God would be *WITH US*.

A challenge for you: "Letting Go"

This challenge is probably the toughest! I remember years ago, when I only had two kids. It seemed like I was constantly worrying about them. I remember my husband saying to me, "Jamie, you have got to entrust your kids to God." Well, I flat out told him "NO! God does not love them as much as I do. He might allow them to have experiences I would never allow them to have." It wasn't until kid number three came along that I realized I didn't have much control at all. I remember the day very vividly that I decided I needed to have faith and give my kids to God. I was driving down the road with my three adorable children in the van. We were crossing over a bridge with a river beneath. I had gone over this bridge with Josh and Kate many times before and the horrifying thought of me losing control and plunging into the river would cross my mind. Then I would strategize in my mind, a plan of how to get the kids unbuckled, hold them both in one arm and use my other arm to swim to shore. Well, when I crossed this river with *three* kids in my van, no matter how hard I tried to figure out a successful escape plan, I was left devastated. I realized then and there, if I wanted to keep my sanity in the years to come, I was going to have to choose to believe that a greater power than me had a plan. That day I told God I would begin trusting him with my children. Now, I knew this didn't guarantee they wouldn't have adversities of their own, but it did help me knowing that my creator loved them more than I knew how. I trusted that no matter what adversities my kids might face, He would be there with them, just as He had always been there for me.

I find it interesting that as parents, we don't want our children to experience certain hardships. And when you think about it, our parents felt the same way about us. Yet, we know that it was our experiences that shaped us into who we are today. We need to understand that it is necessary for *OUR* kids to have their *OWN* experiences in life as well. We must remember, the way to handle adversity is to find value in it. It's important to help our children find the value in their own challenges and learn from them, just as we learned from ours.

Letting Go Challenge: Part 1

Identify an experience that your mother would never have wanted you to go through and write down what you learned and how that experience actually contributed to your progression.

Letting Go Challenge: Part 2

As you watch your kids take on life, teach them to value their adversities as well. That way when life hands them something unexpected and difficult, you can have confidence that they too, will use their adversities as tools, rather than a weapon of defeat. Help them see the lesson that is worth learning.

PART 6

Why God Made Our Kids So Cute
So we wouldn't sell them on Ebay

Oh, please...TELL me that is NOT what I think it is.

By Jamie

My kids and I were in Columbus, Ohio, visiting close friends of ours. The day we were leaving for home, we decided to use our last few hours together shopping at the local thrift store. Today was "half off everything" day! (I know, "half off" at the *thrift store...REALLY?* What can I say? I like to save my pennies!)

Anyway, my friend Reba took Josh in her cart, while I took Kate in mine. Despite the fact that Josh was three at the time, my potty training attempts had been *FUTILE*, and soon we smelled a rather repugnant aroma coming from Josh that told us it was time for a diaper change. So, I did what any *GOOD* parent would do: I decided to grab a *couple* more items and then change his diaper after we had checked out. While I was looking at shirts, I heard Reba's panicked voice say, "Jamie, you need to get over here!" I could see Josh's little head barely sticking up over the clothes rack, and people were staring at him. My first thought was, *Well, seeing that we haven't LOST him, things can't be TOO bad.* I entered the aisle and was confused at what all the fuss was about.

"What?" I asked Reba. She didn't say a word, and with wide eyes she just pointed to the ground. *Oh no, it COULDN'T be. That is NOT what I think it is.* YUP, there was a brown turd staring up at me. Josh had reached into his diaper and was, apparently, amused by the squishy, sticky matter he had discovered. My mouth *dropped* open as I surveyed the entire scene. Not only was there poop on the floor, but it was oozing between his fingers like play-dough and he was smearing it all over the cart as he rubbed his hands up and down the handle bar! I was *MORTIFIED!* Not only was the situation quite *DISGUSTING*, 'cause I don't care *HOW* cute you think your kids are, cleaning their *poo* off of....well, *ANYTHING*...is *disgusting*, but it was also *EMBARRASSING*!!! After all, we were in the middle of a *STORE*!!!! With *PEOPLE* in it!!!! I ran to the van and *DUG* through the suitcase, which was, thankfully, loaded in the van on account of our departure that day. With a pair of clean britches, I *RACED* back into the store, *SWIPED* Josh out of the cart, and carried him at *ARM'S LENGTH* to the bathroom, while the unlucky employee of the month got to mop up the turd. When I was through wiping down every *INCH* of Josh's body, just in case, and all the fecal matter had been scraped out from under his fingernails, I made a really important decision. It was *TIME* to get Josh potty trained!

Hooray! It's picture day... what a Kodak moment.

By Jamie

My first son, Josh, was 16 months old and he hadn't had his first haircut, yet. My husband was *BEGGING* me to cut it, yet I just couldn't bring myself to give up his beautiful curls. However, it really needed to be done; I could actually pull it up on top of his head into a scrunchy. *Eeek!* So, before drastically changing his babyhood into toddlerhood, I decided to get his pictures taken. But *SERIOUSLY*, all the work that goes into "picture day" is enough to make you avoid it *FOREVER*. The adventure started the night before when Josh fell, headfirst, into the corner of the kitchen cabinet. Within moments, a knot began to form, and a big purple line appeared in the *CENTER* of his forehead. *Figures, he hasn't hit his face ALL week, and now that pictures are scheduled for tomorrow he decides to pick a fight with gravity!* Fortunately, Mary Kay and I worked our magic the next day and his battle wound was barely noticeable.

We arrived at the studio late, of course, yet they still managed to squeeze us in. *Whew!* The next twenty minutes were quite tiring and sounded something like this: "Say cheese…Look at the froggy…Sit still…Over here…Nope…Up here…Now look at my hand…Oh, come on, smile," until finally she handed him a teddy bear and he lit right up. *FLASH!* We *GOT* it!

While I went to the checkout to pick out my package and pay, I passed off my son to his Aunt Jess, who, thank goodness, accompanied me that day. There were kids *EVERYWHERE*. It was *CHAOS*. It took me a few minutes to decide which package I wanted to purchase, but, eventually, I handed over my card and signed on the dotted line. While they were processing my order, I looked across the room at Josh to see how he was doing. He seemed to think all these kids were *QUITE* interesting. At just that moment, a little girl caught his eye. She was in a pink dress with cute little white tights, and she was trying her hardest to climb up onto one of the chairs. I thought her little struggle was adorable and entertaining. As I was chuckling, my *CURIOUS* little son came up behind her and pulled her DRESS up to check out her *LACY BLOOMERS!*

Ahhhhh! I was *ALL* the way across the room trying to figure out if I could pretend he wasn't *MINE*. Fortunately, my sister was at the scene of the crime and removed the perpetrator (and *ALSO* looked like the guilty mom! *Wink!*). Things like this always seems to be *FUNNIER* when it is someone *ELSE'S* kid, but *NOPE*, today it was *MINE!* But I covered it well. When we walked out of the studio I gave Jess the raised eyebrow and said, "Seriously, you *GOTTA* keep your son from sneaking peeks at lacy bloomers. Jeesh!"

Still friends?

By Jessica

My life with Jake actually *BEGAN* in the state of Colorado. One would say I picked up my Michigan roots and flew a long way for a "blind date". But, after paying $100 *twice* to postpone my flight and make the "date" last longer, I actually moved to Colorado to hang out with this awesome guy and get to know him better. Well, long story short, we dated for a year, and then I moved back to Michigan to be near my sister, who was expecting kid number *FOUR!* Jake couldn't *LIVE* without me (*wink!*), so he and his U-Haul weren't far behind. (That's the way *I* like to tell the story, anyway!) And now here we are, married with two little boys of our own. What can I say? Some blind dates work out, even if they are 1500 miles away. The only problem is that's how far we have to travel *BACK* to Colorado to visit family and friends, so it *DOESN'T* happen often.

This year, my family went to Denver to have Christmas with Jake's parents. *Yay!* (And that's genuine, by the way—my in-laws are great.) But I was *ALSO* excited because, during our stay, I was able to coordinate a visit with one of my *BEST* friends, Shannon, who I hadn't seen in *TWO* years! Back when we were single with no kids, we would meet on the patio at Starbucks, soaking up the Colorado sun as we dished about our week with our coffee in hand. I knew the visit wasn't going to be the way it used to be. Nope! This would be different, considering our children would be dining with us today. No fancy coffee. This time the location would be Shannon's apartment, and the cuisine would be macaroni and cheese and Kool-Aid. *But it'll STILL be GREAT to catch up,* I thought.

Ayden and Shannon's boy were best buds from the start. *This is going great!* They disappeared into the next room and played the *WHOLE* time. My youngest, on the other hand, was exhausted from the time change and downright *CRANKY*. Much of our conversation was interrupted by, "Zayne don't touch. Zayne don't put that in your mouth! No, you cannot play with the phone...and stay away from the Christmas tree!" And if I wasn't getting him out of trouble, he was in my lap whining. Not *QUITE* the Starbucks patio ambiance.

As the hours passed and the sun began to fade, so did Zayne, 'cause it was his bedtime according to *HIS* time zone. *Wow! Where did the time go?* I reluctantly pried myself off her couch to go tell Ayden to say goodbye to his newfound friend. But when I walked into her son's bedroom where our boys were playing, I just stood there...*IN SHOCK*! Despite the fact that I couldn't see the floor for all the toys, I spotted my son in the middle of the room with a *PAINTBRUSH* in his hand and *LOTS of FRESH RED PAINT* on the end of it! *Oh, no! WHAT has he DONE?!?* I couldn't breathe. I rushed over to him only to find the situation *MUCH WORSE* than what I thought. He held a coloring book *SATURATED* in paint (and *NOT* the washable kid paints you are probably thinking of...it was heavy duty acrylic paint Shannon's son had received for his birthday). I slowly peeled my eyes away from the coloring book, horribly afraid to look around and see what *ELSE* my little "artist" had touched. The paint *DRIPPED* off the edge of the book onto the carpet. *PANIC* set in! Thoughts of grabbing my kid and fleeing the scene *RACED* through my mind! But who was I kidding? We *ALL* know the load-up time of two toddlers; there was *NO* chance of a quick escape!

"SHANNON!!!" I hollered, in hysteria. She came running, and then we both stood there, paralyzed, as we surveyed the damage. *IT WAS AWFUL.* Let me just try to paint the picture here. (No pun intended. Lol.) *Every* possible toy (and I mean *EVERY* toy her son owned) was on the floor. Little Matchbox cars, big trucks, road rugs, books, Legos, action figures, and even those random $1 McDonald's toys our kids refuse to get rid of *ALL* were all strewn about with the blankets and pillows that had been thrown off the bed. *EACH* item had been decorated with *SOME* trace of *RED* paint. Not only was the floor *DOUSED* in paint...so was my son! He stood there not really knowing *WHY* I was so horrified, 'cause apparently he was quite proud of his art. I looked over and saw that Shannon's son *ALSO* had paint on him and was jumping on the bed. *Oh, thank GOODNESS! At least it wasn't just MY kid!* (Yeah, as bad as that sounds, you *all KNOW* you would have been thinking the same thing!)

Shannon and I just stood there, mouths gaping, wondering what to do or even where to start. I was *SICK* to my stomach. I don't know how long we stood there or how many times we kept saying, "Oh...my...gosh." YEAH. I felt like *FRIEND of the YEAR.*

"Ayden, get to the bathroom and clean up," I finally said, as calmly as possible, while trying to get my brain to recall how to tell my legs to move. As I watched him walk out of the bedroom, I noticed little red footprints following him. "AHHHHH!" I scooped him up and *RIPPED* off his socks to wash him up. Even though he was still *STAINED* red, at least paint wasn't *DRIPPING* off his body and onto the floor anymore. Shannon grabbed some 409, and we began cleaning up the tile, which was the *ONLY* thing I was *ABLE* to help her clean because Zayne decided that he was *DONE* for the day and began throwing a fit. Yeah. *THIS* is what I wanted my long lost friend to see...my sons at their *WORST*! As I worked to get Zayne's boots on his rapidly kicking feet, Ayden started crying. Not only was he sad that playtime was over, he noticed I threw away his coloring book he worked *SO* hard to paint. Apparently, he was *QUITE* proud of his masterpiece and was HURT that I tossed it in the trash! Yup...*FRIEND* and *MOM* of the *YEAR*!!!

Whether it was because she was just being *HELPFUL* or trying to get rid of us as fast as *POSSIBLE*, I don't know, but Shannon helped me get my two crying children into the car, and I squeezed her as *HARD* as I could, knowing it would have to last me awhile. As I drove down the highway I felt like the *WORST* friend on the planet. *Hi! How are YOU?? Haven't seen ya in years, but how about I let my children DESTROY your apartment, making SURE you don't get that deposit back?!? And then I'm gonna take off and leave you with the mess!* I cried *ALL* the way back to my in-laws. Honestly, I didn't know if it was because I couldn't do anything to help her or if it was the fact that I wouldn't see her again for a *LONG* time.

I did call Shannon later that week to find out, to my horror and embarrassment, that the paint *NEVER* came out. Thank goodness we are *STILL FRIENDS*...I think. Warm fuzzies every time I think of our visit? Nope, more like a mountain of guilt! And a strong desire to put my little "artist" up for sale on Ebay. (*Wink!*)

Terrible Twos

By Jessica

When I had my first son, I never believed people when they talked about the "terrible twos". Ayden never really hit an unruly stage until he was three, and even then we were always able to reason with him. Now, after having *ZAYNE*, my husband and I could *BOTH* relate with the stories of "terrible twos"! (Ironically, I thought I was struggling with this behavior *BEFORE* he turned two. Little did I know we had only hit the *TIP* of the iceberg!) It started off as whining and proceeded to fit-throwing. And I mean *FIT-THROWING*! We are talking lying on the floor, throwing his feet to and fro, screaming as loud as he could. I would just sit there and stare at him, wondering what demon had found its way into his adorable little body.

Zayne's behavior eventually got so overwhelming that I began staying home. *A LOT.* The supermarket was just *NOT* an option unless I was prepared to listen to him scream the *WHOLE* time. And I don't know many moms out there that would enjoy not only listening to their children scream, but *ALSO* creating a spectacle like a highway accident that nobody can take their eyes off of as they drive by. Most of the time, I really just didn't have it in me to endure the negative judgment.

On one particular day, I was *FORCED* to venture out for Zayne's doctor appointment. The office was about 45 minutes away and near the health food store. Very rarely do I get to the health food store because of the drive, so I decided to take advantage of the fact that we'd be *THAT* close to one. Both my kids and I had been sick for what felt like a whole month, so I was *DETERMINED* to stop and get some children's Echinacea and Golden Root to boost their immune systems. Pulling into the parking lot, I felt like a Navy SEAL psyching himself up for a mission across enemy lines. We go in, grab the goods, and get out. *We go in, grab the goods, and get out!* I kept repeating my chant to keep me focused as I took a deep breath, shut the car off, and walked around to Zayne's door. We walked in, hand-in-hand, while I couldn't help but wonder when the demon would show his face.

To my surprise, Zayne was doing great! He was actually *ADORABLE!* His curls *bouncing* with excitement. His little finger pointing at all the new things. In fact, it looked like he hadn't been out of the house in *MONTHS* from all his enthusiasm. And come to think of it, he *HADN'T!* I plopped him into the cart and up and down the aisles we went. He was so excited! I pushed my cart around the aisles, trying to locate my herbs as quickly as possible and think of anything else I needed to grab. When we passed by the protein shake aisle, I backed up and read a few labels.

"I wanna get out," Zayne said. *Shoot,* I thought, *I've gotten side-*

tracked and now my window of getting in and out without a fit is closing! "Mommy, I wanna get out." He started to pull himself out of the cart seat and I spotted a sample dish with some "healthy" Cheetos in it. *That will work,* I thought. I rushed over and grabbed a *BIG* handful. I knew it would only buy me about two minutes, so I filled his little hand with as many as he could hold and, looking around guiltily, grabbed another big handful for later. I felt like an idiot, but desperate moms call for *DESPERATE MEASURES*! I had *BARELY* stepped away from the snack bin when I noticed Zayne putting the *WHOLE* handful in his mouth. I just looked at him, stunned, because is little lips couldn't even close around all those chips! He had cheese powder all around his mouth and even some in his eyebrows! His little hand was outstretched toward me with now wet, white goo all over it. "More," he said, as puffs of powder sprinkled out of his mouth. *All I could think was, This is the time in war when you have to IGNORE the grenades going off beside you and simply get your MISSION accomplished.* So, I took a deep breath and prepared myself for what needed to be done. I gave him the other handful, bravely walked away from the Cheetos, and entered the herb aisle to quickly begin looking for what I needed. All too soon, his little hand reached out again.

"More." And I *KNEW* the *FIT* was coming.

"No more, Zayne, we are almost done," I said, as excitedly as I could.

"More!" he said again, only louder. I turned away trying to find what I needed. "MORE!!" he screamed this time. I felt the familiar tiredness come over me and decided to simply ignore him. I just wanted to *GET* my things and *GET OUT*. I ignored his tantrum and feverishly tried to read labels to choose exactly what I wanted.

It was somewhere in the midst of the screaming and fit-throwing that a young woman came up to me and asked, "Can I help you find something?"

"MORE MOMMY.....MORE.....MORE SEEEEE-TOTHS!!"

"Um, no... I think I'm good. But, thank you," I said to the girl. I must have looked like I didn't *notice* my child thrashing around in the cart seat while *SCREAMING* at the top of his lungs. I gave her the *sweetest* smile and turned back to my herb hunting. She backed away slowly, giving Zayne a look that let me know she was *NOT* a mom. I finally found liquid Echinacea and grabbed it. But then something *ELSE* caught my eye. Vitamin C combined with Echinacea in one capsule? *WOW!!!! No way!!!!* The young woman was still at the end of the aisle trying to figure out why I was *NOT* dealing with my screaming little boy. I turned to her with excitement and said, "Oh my goodness! I had *NO* idea they made Vitamin C *AND* Echinacea together in *ONE* pill!! It's been *SO* long since I have been out! How exciting!?!"

All the while, Zayne was still ranting, "MOMMY.....MORE! MOMMY! AHHHHHHH! MORE!" The lady gave me a half smile, almost as if she *knew* I had not been out in a while before I even said it.

"This is perfect!" I exclaimed, strolling up to the front of the store. Before I checked out, I looked for my favorite chap-stick and was bummed when I found its box empty. "MOMMY....MOMMY.....MORE!" Zayne's face was stained with tears and red enough to look like he just ran a marathon. *Wow, he is REALLY working it.*

"Are you out of this chap-stick?" I calmly asked a young man working in the aisle.

He looked at Zayne and said, "Excuse me?" while leaning forward trying to hear me over my enthusiastic fit-thrower.

"MOMMY.....MORE MOMMY....MORE SEEEEEE-TOTHS!!!"

I raised my eyebrows, looked the worker square in the eyes, and repeated, "Are you out of this chap-stick?"

He looked horrified at my child and then back at me. "Um.... yeah, I think so."

"SEEEEEEE-TOTHS...MOMMY.....AAHHHHHH...SEEEEEEEE-TOTHS".

"Well, could you check because I live a ways away and want to be sure." I could feel my sweet smile turning into a smile that the men in white coats would give me medication for. He walked away, and I headed for the checkout. The older lady at the register looked at Zayne and smiled...*SINCERELY*.

"Is he two?" she asked. *FINALLY*, someone who *KNEW* my pain. Someone who *UNDERSTOOD* what it's like to just be *SO* overwhelmed, yet knows that life *MUST* go on. Someone who didn't JUDGE me, but better yet, *FELT* for me.

"Yes...he is." My voice almost cracked.

"Awe, look at those curls." Her smile was warm. His screams and kicking didn't seem to faze her. She leaned over and gave Zayne a sucker. "Here ya go! These are my favorite!" Zayne stopped screaming for the first time in 20 minutes and smiled at her.

"Thucker Mommy!"

"Yup," I said, feeling like my son won the fight, but *GLAD* someone *ELSE* gave in. The young man returned (to my surprise, honestly) and informed me there was no more chap-stick. So I paid for my herbs, pulled my *sticky* son out of the cart, and headed home. Mission accomplished, with only *MINOR* casualties! (Nothing a hot bath couldn't take care of!)

A day at the Supermarket with Bo
By Jamie

Bo was in one of his "have to be the boss and drive my mom crazy" moods. I was in my "get what we need as fast as possible and get out of here" moods. While I was pushing my cart through the grocery store with my list and pen in hand, Bo kept ripping my list out of my hand and then, of course, he would try and take the pen as well. At first, I would just pull my hand away from the cart, but (as you may know) a cart full of groceries and a kid is hard to steer one-handed. I caved and just gave him the list and pen, relying on my memory, in hopes of getting out of the store as quickly as possible.

A few aisles after giving up my pen, I caught Bo drawing on his arms!

I *SNATCHED* the pen away and the *SCREAMING* began, followed by the hitting and kicking, which of course attracted *MANY* stares. I grabbed Bo's hand to keep him from hitting me, and he screamed even louder, so I let go, and he hit me again. A "win/win" solution seemed impossible...for *ME* anyway. He was obviously "winning" at something, no matter *WHAT* I did!

Later, after the feud had calmed, the groceries began to pile up in the cart. Bo saw this as an opportunity to better familiarize himself with the concept of *gravity*. He began reaching back and tossing items out of the cart. *Right, because picking our things up off the floor while trying to steer the cart is SO much fun!* I would say, "No, Bo!" and while I was bending over to pick the item up, I would hear *ANOTHER* hit the floor. It had become a game of fetch. *So exhausting.* By this time, I was ready to take the frozen pizza box he threw out of my cart and WHOP him on the *HEAD* with it! I figured a little "induced coma" might speed up my shopping trip. (Don't worry, I'm kidding. I wouldn't want social services knocking on my door. Lol! I do *LOVE* him. He is just *INCREDIBLY* annoying in the supermarket.)

Bo finally stopped throwing various items out of the cart (thank God for miracles!) and I was able to resume shopping. I headed for the school supplies, seeing how summer break was coming to an end and it was time to buy supplies once again. Trying to stick to a *tight* budget, I took the time to search for the *BEST* deal. As I was staring at three-ring binders, wondering to myself, *Why are the girly ones on sale, when my boy is the one who needs one?* My annoyance with the store pricing was soon interrupted by another fellow shopper who had stopped to ask, "Um, is he *supposed* to be opening your *markers?*"

I looked at Bo and saw he had ripped open the package of markers and was throwing them on the floor, one by one, being sure to remove the cap first. "Oh, my gosh!" I gasped, as I frantically picked all of the markers up from the floor and pried the remaining two out of his strong-willed, little hand. *Now I am DONE!* I said, to myself, as I swerved my cart into the nearest checkout lane.

On our way out the door, my son was again screaming because he was mad and was creating another scene. People were turning their heads to see whose blaring child was coming their way. All I could think was, *"It's mine!"* I was so embarrassed. I was *DEFINITELY* contemplating selling this kid on Ebay.

Later, after arriving home, I put *Curious George* in charge of entertaining Bo. I began reviewing some of the "Value Based Parenting" principles I am certified to teach other parents. It was time to "practice what I preach." I had been allowing Bo to get away with these shenanigans *ALL* summer, and with my older three going back to school next week, it was time to "Take back the grocery store."

Once the kids returned to school, I planned to teach Bo how to shop! I picked a warm, sunny day when I had *PLENTY* of time so that my stress and anxiety would stay low. I knew that one of the most important variables that would affect how successful my teaching exercise would be was the energy I was carrying during the process. I have learned that our kids can feel our stress and, as a result, it shows in their behavior. Whether it is the stress of accomplishing our required tasks or simply the pressure we put on ourselves by worrying how we look to others, our kids *FEEL* it. Many times we are too concerned about what *ALL* the other parents are thinking when our child is misbehaving. We see the stares and *ASSUME* they are judging our parenting skills when, in fact, the only people who may be placing judgment are those who don't have kids of their own and therefore have *NO* idea what they are in for when they become parents themselves! As for the experienced parents, they're probably thinking, "Yup, been there, done that."

As I began the mission of the day—teaching Bo to grocery shop—I knew my success was directly connected to how well I let go of my fear of what others would think of me during the process. So, with determined energy (and a fru fru coffee, I'm not gonna lie!), I said a quick prayer and I ventured back to the supermarket with Bo. It was either *THAT* or *STARVE* my three other children. I am pretty sure, as parents, feeding the kids is a requirement.

And so I began step one of my new course of action. Just outside the supermaket doors, I knelt down eye-level with Bo and told him *EXACTLY* what I expected of him and *EXACTLY* what his consequence would be in the event he didn't listen. "Bo!" I said sternly, "If you scream, throw groceries out of my cart, or just plain don't listen, then you will be going back to the van for a time out." Once he verbally agreed, we entered the store. And that's when the *magic* happened (insert dreamy smile).

Well, not *QUITE*. We made it through the doors and over to the carts, where Bo had his first protest. Apparently, I had chosen the *WRONG* cart and he was refusing to ride in it. "Ok, let's go take a time out!" As we walked out I smiled confidently at the greeter and said, "We will be back in a minute."

While we headed for the door, Bo seemed to be proudly thinking, "Well I showed her!" because he seemed quite happy to be leaving. However, when I strapped him in his seat without any toys, movies, or snacks, he began to complain. After a couple minutes, I asked him if he was ready to go back into the store and listen. When he agreed, I reminded him of the procedure once again, and back in for round two we went! *Oh, YEAH*, I had my *GAME* face on. And *THAT'S* when the magic happened? Well...

As we entered the store for the *SECOND* time, we didn't even *MAKE* it to the carts. He caught sight of the candy dispensers and *INSISTED* on me giving him a quarter. Of course, when my answer was, "No," the second fit was displayed. Once again, I smiled at the greeter and walked out of the store to repeat the time-out process. This time he decided to play his own game, and when I asked if he was ready to go back in his first response was, "No." Being the smart mom I am, I decided *TWO* could play *THAT* game. I said, "Okay, let me know when you are ready." And I began cleaning my van. (No sense wasting any time; might as well be productive!) While he sat in time out, I threw out the stale goldfish and French fries that were all over the van floor. After a few more minutes, Bo decided his game just wasn't paying off and agreed to cooperate. And *THAT'S* when the magic happened! (Okay, I can tell you don't even believe me by now.)

The *THIRD* time we went back into the store I *DID* manage to get him buckled into the cart and complete a *PORTION* of my shopping before he started screaming for the grapes I put into the cart and refused to give to him at the time. Taking a much-needed deep breath, while reminding myself that he looks like me and he is *REALLY* cute when he sleeps, I smiled calmly at the greeter and then left my cart of just a few groceries with her and headed for the van to repeat the process...*AGAIN*. (I'm not even going to talk about magic here.)

The fourth time back into the store we *FINALLY* started to cover some ground. I was *JUST* about finished when the groceries piled up to his reach. He grabbed a bag of popcorn and mischievously held it over the side of the cart. "Don't drop that out of the cart or you will have to go back to time out," I warned. He played around a little, putting it in the basket and then holding it out again. While he amused himself, wanting to get a reaction out of me, I simply continued shopping. And then... he *DROPPED* it. I felt the emotion of being overwhelmed begin to *FLOOD* through my body. Thoughts of selling him on Ebay flashed through my mind! *HOW many TIMES are we going to go BACK to the van?* Nevertheless, I took a deep breath and reminded myself that all this consistency *WOULD* pay off. Granted, he was a *LOT* more stubborn than my first three, but hey, it's this type of commitment that will serve him well as an adult, right?! (Lol!) When I left my cart with the greeter, *AGAIN*, I giggled underneath my breath. This *HAD* to be quite the sight for her.

Finally, our *FIFTH* time back into the store we were able to finish shopping. The *magic REALLY happened!* Bo was so sweet for the remainder of the time. At the checkout, he grabbed a candy bar off the shelf, and when I told him, "No," and asked him to put it back, he *LISTENED.* I was *SO* excited. We checked out and I grabbed some change to let him ride the mechanical pony ride.

As I walked out, I could *FEEL* the *DIFFERENCE* in Bo. I felt *PROUD* of myself! I stayed calm and stuck to the mission. He had learned a lot today, and it really was sort of a magical moment for both of us. As I walked to my car, I had to laugh just thinking of the look on the greeter's face the fourth and fifth time I left her with my cart. Although, as crazy as I may have seemed, I am *SURE* she preferred to babysit my cart as opposed to the alternative of hearing those infamous words, "Cleanup in aisle six," 'cause some kid threw the grape jam out of the cart. Not that *I* would *KNOW* what it's like to have a kid throw grape jam out of the cart. (*Wink*! Lol!) Nope, the Ebay sale is cancelled...for today.

Hmmmm...is Anger Management in Ayden's future?
By Jessica

Last weekend, my friend Rachel and her son Luke spent the day at my house. We were upstairs chatting in my bedroom while our three-year-old boys played in the toy room down the hall. Not but a couple minutes into catching up, I heard Luke crying. I automatically assumed my child had done something to him. You might think this rather insensitive of me, but recently Ayden had developed *QUITE* the hitting habit. Although we were working on it, I felt like we had the same "why it's not nice to hit people" talk every other day. As soon as I walked in the room I saw the grin on his face that told me he was guilty. (I tried not to laugh.)

"What happened?" I asked.

"Wuke is crwying," Ayden responded, with a shrug of his shoulders.

"Yeah, I can see that. *Why* is he crying?" I asked, curtly.

"Yup, he is." Ayden didn't seem to comprehend the question *why* too well.

"What did you do, Ayden?" I rephrased my question.

He looked up from the toy he was playing with and matter-of-factly said, "I hit him." And then went *RIGHT* back to playing as if he simply told me what he wanted for lunch rather than telling me he assaulted his friend.

"You hit him?" I asked.

"Yup I did...on da head...wike dis." He proceeded to demonstrate with his little hand, as he whopped himself on the forehead. Hiding my giggle at how blatantly honest and straightforward he was, I (of course) began reciting the talk of "why we don't hit our friends on the head", a concept I didn't think was *THAT* hard to grasp. When Luke returned to the room, Ayden apologized. All was well.

So, I went back down the hall to restart girl-time with my friend. I kid you *NOT*, about seven minutes later I heard Luke crying...*AGAIN*. As I stomped down the hall back to the toy room, Luke passed by me with big crocodile tears running down his face. As I entered the room once again, Ayden was just playing with his toys as if nothing had happened.

"Ayden?" I said with frustration and confusion in my voice.

"Yup, I did," he answered.

Again, I had to hold back the laughter at his candor. Even though he already answered, I felt compelled to ask anyway, "Did you hit Luke?"

"Yup."

"Why?"

"Yup, I did," he answered, again with no comprehension of the word *why*. "I hit Wuke on da head wike dis, wif dis toy." He picked up a squirt gun and hit himself on the head to demonstrate once again.

While I am not a fan of the hitting, his candid replay of the whole scene WAS funny. This kid was TOO cute for his own good.

"Ayden, what did I say about hitting our friends?"

"Mommy, I didn't hit him wif my hand...I hit him wif a toy," he said to me, with a "Duh, mom!" look on his face. In his little brain, the two acts were QUITE different.

So I clarified. "Do not hit with your hands. Do not hit with toys. Not in a house, not with a mouse. Not in a box, not with a fox. Do not hit here or there. Do NOT hit ANYWHERE. Don't do anything that will hurt someone else. OKAY?" I said in exasperation.

He looked up from his toy, not amused with my Dr. Suess impression, and said so simply, "Okay." And went back to playing.

I couldn't help but laugh as I told my friend what Ayden said to me in the toy room. And, yes, about four minutes later we heard Luke crying... AGAIN! I walked into the room and saw Ayden shutting the door to the toy room. He looked up at me with that same guilty grin.

"Ayden, did you hit Luke again?" I asked, exasperated.

"Nope!" That's all he said. He just stood there looking at me with a smile on his adorable, but GUILTY, face.

"What did you do?"

Not only did my son fess up to the crime, but he ACTED it out for me again. He opened the door to the toy room and began shutting out the light. "I shut da wite out wike dis and I shut da door," he said, as he slammed the door shut and then looked up at me again with a sort of "Job well done" smile. Keep in mind, our toy room is actually a small walk-in closet, with no windows.

"Ayden, did you shut Luke in the toy room with the lights out?" I asked, to make *SURE* I had understood the specifics.

"Yup!" he answered confidently, as he nodded his head. Despite the trauma my little trouble-maker was causing, it was all I could do to keep from bursting into laughter! I tried to think like a three-year-old. He was told *NOT* to hit with his hands, so he hit him with a toy. Then he was told *NOT* to hit with his hand or toys, so he decided to shut him in the small, dark toy room...because that's *NOT* hitting. (Insert sly, towheaded boy grinning.) I can see how each offense seems *DIFFERENT* to a three-year-old; I am now just wondering if I should be worried about a future career as the schoolyard bully!

Aren't they angels...when they sleep?
By Jamie

It's the end of another busy day in the "Hood" (motherhood, that is), and all of my kids are *finally* tucked in bed. I've now returned to the kitchen for the final cleanup. I pick the remaining smashed peas and corn out of the carpet and wipe off the sticky highchair. I pull a few goldfish crackers out from between the couch cushions and am tempted to eat them, until I get distracted by the squished brown banana under the table. As I wash the last of the splattered milk off the kitchen cupboards, I breathe a *sigh* of *RELIEF*. I continue down the hall and toss a few toys into the toy box, then head upstairs to check on the sleeping kids. I can't turn in until I have caressed each of their foreheads with one more mother's kiss to last them through the night.

When I open the door to each of their rooms and step inside, I can't help but notice the peace that permeates the still room. Warm affection wells up inside me as I look down on each of their precious little faces, wrapped in what seems to be *angelic* rest. As I stand there in a gazing trance, I find myself trying to memorize all of their little features because I *KNOW* they are sure to change by morning. I *gently* put their miniature hands in mine and stare at each *tiny* finger. During the summer months, I often get a peek at their stubby toes and chubby thighs *sprawled* out over the mattress. I'm once again *amazed* by their pint-sized breaths in and out through their small open mouths. I thank God for the precious gift of life He has entrusted to Michael and me. I gently *kiss* them, and then pry myself away so I can get the rest I need for the next day, when these *angels* sleep *no more*.

A challenge for you: "Commendable Kids" List

Postpone the Ebay sale! The truth of the matter is, as exhausting as our kids can be at times, we really wouldn't trade them for the world! I'm closing this book with the task of looking at your kid's "Awesomeness"! I encourage you to focus on what makes them so amazing! I like to tell parents that their kid's greatest weakness is also their greatest strength. Now, this may be my own survival technique for dealing with my own *stubborn* child. (Lol!) You've gotta figure though, if my kid won't take no for an answer now without a ton of consistency and discipline on my part, then I can be confident that while he is chasing his dreams, as an adult, and others tell him, "No, you can't!" Those words won't stop him then either. Lol   I obviously have added some humor, but there is truth in my statement. Set a goal for the next few days to pay attention to your kids "Awesomeness"! Noticing the "strength" of their "weaknesses" will help us see the value in their character qualities, even when we have to deal with their misbehavior. This could lead to many great conversations with your kid as they grow, empowering them to see their own value as they learn and progress.

Create a "Commendable Kids" List

Make a list of some of your kid's *Awesome* attributes. Look at what might be one of your kids "shortcomings" and define how it will also serve as their greatest strength.

Weakness	Transformed to	Strength
Too emotional with people		Kind-hearted, emotional connection
Stubborness		A never give up attitude

Weakness	Transformed to	Strength

1. _____

2. _____

3. _____

4. _____

5. _____

About the Authors

Jamie Lightner married her high school sweetheart and is blessed with four amazing children who have provided her with plenty of source material for her many adventures in motherhood. She began writing twelve years ago to find the "funny" in "spilt milk" because, when you have kids, messes of all kinds are just part of life. Jamie is also a life coach through TurningLeaf Wellness Center and has a passion for helping people believe in themselves and truly enjoy the many adventures of life. For more information on parenting workshops or private coaching sessions with Jamie visit:

www.jamielightner.com.

Jessica Warren was set up on a blind date 1500 miles from her small Michigan hometown and she was crazy enough to go! After falling madly in love in Colorado, she dragged her husband-to-be back to Michigan, where they married and started their own adventures in parenting. There is never a dull day with her two beautiful towheads. While she helps her older son through his first year of school, she is walking her youngest through chemo in a fight against a brain tumor. Through it all, she sees God's blessing and is thankful for all that she's been given.

Made in the USA
Monee, IL
21 August 2020